Praise for *Ancestral Energy Healing*

"Scientific research from CDC and other reputable organizations now confirms ancestral trauma is held within our DNA. In *Ancestral Energy Healing*, Dr. Shelley Kaehr shows readers how to transform this energy and move into a brighter future. The exercises should be a real benefit to those who use them."

—**GEORGE NOORY,** host of *Coast to Coast AM* and *Beyond Belief*

"Dr. Shelley Kaehr's Genealogical Regression is one of the most fascinating processes I've heard of in years....Shelley teaches people to identify the exact places within the body where their ancestors still live, so they can send light to those areas for healing and transformation. Her groundbreaking work will become a lasting and important contribution to the growing literature and teachings on this important topic."

—**LISA BONNICE,** host of The Shift Network's *Ancestral Healing Summit* and author of *Castle Gate*

"In her groundbreaking book and clinical work, Dr. Kaehr guides us through the processes of healing ancient trauma wounds and releasing them from being trapped in our lives and bodies. Dr. Kaehr's writing is clear, easy to follow, and it's like having her right in the same room with you when you do the exercises. This book can change your life and root out pains and patterns that have been festering deep inside. I highly recommend you read it and work the processes to feel better and freer than you have ever felt in this lifetime."

—**DR. KAC YOUNG,** author of *The Rainbow Witch*

"In *Ancestral Energy Healing*, Dr. Shelley Kaehr shows readers how to identify their ancestors within themselves and send light to those areas using their inner wisdom. Her guidance on pendulums as one of the tools to help in the process is priceless and will help readers transform generations of difficulties and ultimately bring greater joy to themselves and future generations."

—**LANA GENDLIN,** author of *Pendulums & Intuitic*

T0034803

"In her latest book, *Ancestral Energy Healing*, Dr. Shelley Kaehr uses the wisdom of muscle testing with the body and pendulum, along with many other tools to help readers learn how to locate the ancestors within and transform the heavy burdens of the past to create greater joy and peace in life. Deep healing is available to all of us, and Shelley beautifully outlines the path. Highly recommended."
—**KARINA MULLER**, author of *Pendulums & Intuition*

Ancestral
ENERGY
Healing

About the Author

For over twenty years, Shelley A. Kaehr, PhD, has worked with thousands of people around the world, helping them achieve greater peace and happiness in their lives. A renowned past-life regressionist and one of the world's leading authorities on energy healing and mind-body medicine, her award-winning books have been translated into multiple languages around the world.

A spiritual historian, Shelley enjoys creating content to help readers and students remember their soul histories and past lives. She coined the term *Supretrovie* to describe spontaneously induced past-life memories and strives to develop new methods to help people resolve challenging issues that arise from these influences. She created the groundbreaking Genealogical Regression to help seekers resolve inherited ancestral trauma, as well as several energy healing techniques. She believes we all have the power to rewrite our stories and create the life of our dreams.

Visit Shelley online: https://pastlifelady.com.

Ancestral ENERGY Healing

.. • ..

A Guidebook

.. • ..

SHELLEY A. KAEHR PhD

Llewellyn Publications
Woodbury, Minnesota

FIRST EDITION
First Printing, 2024

Cover design by Kevin R. Brown
Interior art by the Llewellyn Art Department

Llewellyn Publications is a registered trademark of Llewellyn Worldwide Ltd.

Library of Congress Cataloging-in-Publication Data (Pending)
ISBN: 978-0-7387-7769-6

Llewellyn Worldwide Ltd. does not participate in, endorse, or have any authority or responsibility concerning private business transactions between our authors and the public.

All mail addressed to the author is forwarded but the publisher cannot, unless specifically instructed by the author, give out an address or phone number.

Any internet references contained in this work are current at publication time, but the publisher cannot guarantee that a specific location will continue to be maintained. Please refer to the publisher's website for links to authors' websites and other sources.

Llewellyn Publications
A Division of Llewellyn Worldwide Ltd.
2143 Wooddale Drive
Woodbury, MN 55125-2989
www.llewellyn.com

Printed in the United States of America

Also by Shelley A. Kaehr, PhD

Heal Your Ancestors to Heal Your Life:
The Transformative Power of Genealogical Regression

Journeys through the Akashic Records:
Accessing Other Realms of Consciousness for Healing and Transformation

Past Lives in Ancient Lands & Other Worlds:
Understand Your Soul's Journey Through Time

The Goddess Discovered:
Exploring the Divine Feminine Around the World

Acknowledgments

This book is dedicated to all my readers and students who have answered the call of their souls to assist their ancestors and humanity in evolving the pain of the past.

Words cannot express my profound gratitude and appreciation for my incredible team at Llewellyn. Thank you for believing in me and my offbeat ideas and for giving me a perfect venue to explore such a wide range of topics. This book would not exist without the support and friendship of my beloved friend Kat Neff. Thank you, Kat! I am also in complete awe of the incredibly talented and supportive Heather Greene, who worked with me on *The Goddess Discovered,* and whose expertise and vision I value so much. I send my love and gratitude to the rest of Llewellyn's amazing team, including Bill Krause, Terry Lohmann, Anna Levine, Sami Sherratt, Alisha Bjorklund, Markus Ironwood, Nanette Stearns, Oxana Schroeder, Katie Stark, Aundrea Foster, Shannon McKuhen, Leah Madsen, and Donna Burch-Brown.

Deepest gratitude to my friends Jim Merideth, Pat Moon, Paula Wagner, Janine, Damaris, Maya, Theresa, Bob, Maria, Lori, Lynn, Sandy, LaRee, James, Susan, Alan and Patsy, and others who do not like to be publicly acknowledged, but who mean so much to me. Heartfelt thanks to everyone at The Shift Network for their support of my Genealogical Regression practice and especially to my dear friend, Lisa Bonnice. Special thanks to Cyndi Dale, George Noory, Dr. Raymond Moody, Linda Moulton Howe, and Dr. Kac Young. Finally, to my readers, thank you for reading my books through these many years. I pray this book helps you on your path to peace, joy, and happiness.

Disclaimer

This book is not intended as a substitute for consultation with a licensed medical or mental health professional. The reader should regularly consult a physician or mental health professional in matters relating to their health and particularly with respect to any symptoms that may require diagnosis or medical attention. This book provides content related to educational, medical, and psychological topics. As such, use of this book implies acceptance of this disclaimer.

Names and identifying details have been changed to protect the privacy of individuals.

Contents

Part Three
....
Ancestral Energy Healing

Exercises

CHAPTER EIGHT

Journal Prompts

CHAPTER EIGHT

Foreword

Like most of us, I studied history in school. I'm sure you've heard one of the reasons it's important to investigate the past.

If you understand history, you don't have to repeat it.

Since becoming an energy healer and author, I understand the accuracy—and incompletion—of that statement.

The truth is that we *are* our history. Yesterday creates today, and today determines tomorrow. Once we understand what has forged who we are, we can break the cycles that are weighing us down.

We can go one better than that, however.

As shared by Shelley Kaehr, PhD, in her revelatory and empowering book *Ancestral Energy Healing*, we don't have to only accept or reject our personal histories. We can change and *heal* yesteryear. By doing so, we can finally and fully embody our true selves.

I invite you to read that last paragraph again. Let it settle into your body and mind. The idea of transforming times past is not only the stuff of science fiction. What sounds fantastical has become hard-core science.

One of the most exciting developments in medical and social science is the discipline of *epigenetics*. This is the study of the *epigenome*, a collection of chemical compounds and proteins that connect to the DNA. Basically, this soup can turn your genes on and off.

Research is suggesting that these compounds carry information from your ancestors' lives. Encoded might be the equivalent of what your grandma felt during a hard time, or a famine endured by your great-granddad. These substances can establish your vulnerability to disease, addictions, allergies, and even relationship choices. They can impact your joys and anxieties, taste buds and deep passions. Mainly, the influences occur when triggered by events in your environment that include everything from climatic stressors to food additives, from another's kindness to the world's cruelties.

A few years ago, researchers stapled a new term onto those already making waves. It seems that these ancestral codes can even pass down *intergenerational trauma.*

What? You can literally inherit suffering from an ancestor—and then undergo similar emotional and mental pain?

Many investigators now support this rather shocking but rather practical concept. I'm an expert in energetics, and I completely buy in. We've long known that everything is made of energy. That includes the visible and invisible parts of 3D reality. Most of this energy, however, is subtle or intangible. When I say "most," I mean 99.999 percent.[1] Why wouldn't the situations our parents or grandparents went through transfer into and shape us? In fact, certain members of the British royal family are explaining the issues they have faced based on that concept.[2]

In the end, your epigenome is like a language, the equivalent to a siren song from the past that sings in your own bones. Those notes play your genes like piano keys, helping you adjust to this incredibly uncertain world.[3]

---

1. Sundermier, "99.9999999% of Your Body Is Empty Space."

2. Cowan-Jenssen, "Prince Harry, Therapy, and Intergenerational Trauma."

3. Spinney, "Epigenetics, the Misunderstood Science That Could Shed New Light on Ageing."

All this science is incredible, but also overwhelming. I would imagine you're asking yourself a very vital question. *How can I ever recover from the generations of trauma, disease, and emotional maladies I've inherited?*

The answers are in this book.

Shelley shares them. Astutely. Interactively. Uniquely.

As she points out, the past, present, and future are interconnected. (Yup, she's quoting scientific data.) What this means is that if your ancestors can sway you, then you can also impact them, or at least the energetics and chemistry you've inherited from them.

As I've stated, the purpose of Shelley's book is learning how to send healing energies to your forebearers. Through this act of power and compassion, you can impressively improve your own life—and the lives of the next generation. The ideas and practices in this book are even more full-bodied than that, however.

As Shelley reveals, you have a soul. You *are* a soul, a being whose existence is profound and endless. Through Shelley's acumen, you'll also be graciously invited to revisit the past, and journey into the future, to activate your own extraordinary soul gifts, such as intuitive and healing faculties.

What might your life become if *all* of you were brought online? If an ability you used during a past life a thousand years ago, supplemented by a potential success in your own future, could be activated in the here and now? Think of the destiny afforded you!

Only Shelley can serve as your guide in this process, as she is *the* expert extraordinaire. As a master past-life regressionist and energy healer, she has shown the path of progress for untold thousands through her client work, podcasts, books, and workshops. Major figures in the spiritual, energy, and self-help disciplines turn to her work to explain how a person's ancestry and their soul can be embraced and transformed for higher purposes.

For me personally, I follow and apply Shelley's work because I so deeply admire her. She showcases integrity. Her insights are incomparable.

The beautiful stuff of her knowledge has fashioned joyful transformation in my own life, and I only hope that you allow her knowledge to perform that same and wonderful sort of alchemy within you.

With your own light brighter and stronger, imagine what a brilliant torch of goodness you can uphold for this entire planet.

—Cyndi Dale

Introduction

Since antiquity, ancestral veneration has played a major role in the lives of humans around our planet, stretching across all continents and all walks of life. Despite that, the modern Western world seemed to have forgotten the importance and reverence that many cultures see as necessity. Now that perspective has changed.

As recently as five years ago, if you had told me that Ancestral Healing was going to become a global phenomenon, I'm not sure I would have believed you. For years, I believed past-life influences affected us daily in profound and often difficult ways. While I still hold that belief, I now recognize that another factor plays perhaps an even more important role in how we feel in our bodies in our current incarnations—ancestral connections. Scientific evidence is making that fact difficult to ignore, especially since new research suggests your ancestors live in your DNA. The connection is real.

Twenty years ago, when I created the Genealogical Regression process, that revelation had not yet been revealed. Despite the evidence or science to back me up, I realized many of the people who came to see me for a past-life regression needed much more than a trip into other lifetimes. Many could not possibly access their past lives until some current-life healing happened first. Many times, that healing needed to occur with parents. Some of these parents were still alive, some were not known in the person's current life, while others were estranged from their parents, adopted, raised by foster families, and everything in between. This led me to evolve the process into conversations where the client could encounter the Higher Selves or soul essences of their parents. Often forgiveness was exchanged, and both the client and the parent expressed a need to send light and healing to their ancestors on one or both sides of their family tree. Thus, the Genealogical Regression process was born.

In the early days, now over twenty years ago, this kind of journey was something I did rarely. Now, it's incredibly common and I've had a chance to reflect on some of the differences between past-life regression and Genealogical Regression.

Ancestral energy healing is not for the faint of heart. Anytime you go into the storehouse of your inner mind to heal the past, issues come up and are hopefully resolved and transformed. When I received my very first full past-life regression to heal unresolved grief I suffered after the death of a friend, it was tough to do and proved incredibly emotional. Likewise, over the years of working with so many people, regressions can be emotional for anybody, depending on what they're working to resolve.

More recently, while putting this book together, I underwent a very deep and personal Ancestral Healing of my own. This journey proved to be so challenging, I experienced firsthand how much harder Ancestral Energy Healing is than the work I did to resolve and find peace in my past lives. Time is strange, however, so I will admit that could simply be because my past-life epiphanies happened so long ago; perhaps I don't fully recall the depths of my emotions as well.

Once I began working with students and clients using the techniques you will explore in this book, I confirmed exactly how difficult Ancestral Energy Healing really is after observing my students' and clients' reactions. People who have done a lot of inner work on themselves even found some of these exercises incredibly challenging, as I did.

I've spent considerable time contemplating this phenomenon and wondering why that is the case, and I've come up with a few ideas to explain why this happens. When you go into your previous incarnations during a guided past-life regression, you use your inner mind to see out of your own eyes and sense the life you had long ago. The typical reaction to that process is a feeling of making things up because often the experiences are far outside of your current-life awareness. When you do Genealogical Regression, you float into the past and explore things that happened to your ancestors. These people are real. The historical events people visit during a Genealogical Regression are real. Not that past lives aren't real—I believe they are; however, your ancestors are documented souls whose existence can be proven. They're not mere figments of your imagination, or some idea you have about who you might have been in your prior incarnation. Whether you believe in reincarnation or not, proving who you were in a past life is nearly impossible. Finding real evidence of your ancestors' existence online or in a box of family heirlooms is a fact. The reality of identifying those who would be on the receiving end of your well wishes and healing makes this personal.

There is a tendency within the kindhearted nature of most people to feel more for others than they feel for themselves. Human nature causes us to empathize with suffering and the plight of others. For all these reasons, working with your ancestors is an emotional journey, as you will soon discover. Back in the early days of my career, I found only a few people needed this kind of healing. Now, thanks to the widespread global shift in consciousness, I can now say with great certainty that during the extraordinary times we're living in, focusing on healing your ancestors is every bit as important as discovering your past lives, if not more so. This book will help you dive into Ancestral Healing processes that I know can change your life for the better, thanks to results I've seen with people all over the world. I'm glad you're here.

Ancestral Healing Finds the Western World

An awakening is happening in Western culture about the ever-growing collective calling to heal our ancestors. I am one who feels drawn to answer that call, and I assume since you're reading this book, you are another such person. Congratulations on answering the call. I truly believe Ancestral Healing work will benefit humanity and future generations.

The context in which much of the current Ancestral Healing movement is framed is widely centered on the idea of healing generational trauma, releasing the energetic blueprints of the horrors that our ancestors have somehow cursed us with and that we are boldly choosing to transform on behalf of our forebears. No doubt, generational curses are alive and well. Our ancestors messed up, offended others—or, perhaps even worse, killed others—and God only knows what else, and now, we, the unfortunate descendants, are the recipients of a tainted legacy and are sadly paying the price for their actions. These traumatic legacies can originate from any number of scenarios. Our ancestors could be the cause of strife for others, or they might be on the receiving end of abuse from other people and subsequently wound up damaged, harmed, killed, or oppressed. Regardless of how things happened, no doubt hardships occurred, and modern people feel the pain of the past. The belief that our ancestors doomed us through these various hardships, and that even with our best efforts it will take generations to improve our circumstances, is quite common and pervasive, and science backs this up.

Epigenetics is the study of how our physiology shifts and changes due to our environment. This expanding field is fundamental to Ancestral Healing because science is now able to show that our traits and vulnerability to stress and anxiety are passed down from our parents.[4] People whose ancestors lived through unspeakable trauma have far higher levels of stress hormones called cortisol in their systems. One of the most transformative studies by Dr. Rachel Yehuda proved that DNA was altered in the children of Holocaust survivors.[5] Science shows the

---

4. Paro, Grossniklaus, Santoro, and Wutz, *Introduction to Epigenetics*, 2.

5. Yehuda, Schmeidler, Wainberg, Binder-Brynes, and Duvdevani, "Vulnerability to Post-traumatic Stress Disorder in Adult Offspring of Holocaust Survivors," 1163–1171.

descendants of Holocaust survivors experience an increased likelihood of struggling with various diseases due to an increase in stress hormones.[6] Whether the stress is passed on from the mother, father, or both, or whether the inclinations toward depression and anxiety happen after the child is born, remains to be seen, yet the conclusion is that offspring of traumatized people have a greater likelihood of experiencing anxiety and depression than other people. From there, more studies continue to reaffirm the conclusion that we are indeed carrying the burdens of our ancestors within us as certain diseases are expressed within our bodies. Studies are cited by reputable sources, including the Centers for Disease Control and Prevention in the United States.

Likewise, other studies suggest that up to 50 percent of our personalities come straight through to us from our ancestors.[7] This means all those cute and quirky little foibles you've had your whole life are actually not just you. They belong to your ancestors, and you are acting them out in your current lifetime.

Another group studied descendants of people who survived the Dutch Hunger Winter during World War II. The study showed that people who experienced malnutrition in utero, when their parents nearly starved to death during this terrible time in history, were more likely to experience a barrage of health challenges in life, and were less successful and maintained a lower socioeconomic status during their lives.[8] The studies in these areas are ongoing and I expect will only increase in number as the years go on and we begin to understand ourselves better than ever before. While I am pleased that such studies are expanding to help us understand the depth to which we are influenced by our ancestral heritage, I'm also left wondering about all the other currently undocumented hardships people around the world have endured since the beginning of time, including the suffering of enslaved

6. Rakoff, "A Long-Term Effect of the Concentration-Camp Experience."

7. Sanchez-Roige et al., "The Genetics of Human Personality," e12439.

8. Ramirez and Haas, "Windows of Vulnerability," 959–989.

peoples, Indigenous populations, women beaten and abused, soldiers who suffered wounds in battles. The possibilities are a bit daunting, and yet the research is moving in the right direction to help humanity heal. All of this is to say that there is no doubt *we inherit our family trauma.* The question remains: *What are we going to do about it?*

How to Use This Book

I believe wholeheartedly in using guided imagery and energy healing methods to assist body, mind, and spirit in transmuting the ill effects of our genetic heritage or any other challenges we face in life. I wrote this book to help you do just that. In the coming pages, you will explore and experience all the techniques I've developed over the years to help my clients overcome challenging chapters in their lineages.

Explore in Your Own Time

Ancestral Healing is a slow but profound process. The journey can be not only powerful, but painful and even emotionally draining. You will go through a series of powerful exercises in the coming chapters, each building upon the priors. You may find that you simply cannot do some of this material, and that's okay. Put the book down and resume when you feel guided to do so.

When I put books like these together, I try to consider a logical form for the exercises and processes. That said, because this work has the potential to be so very challenging, you don't necessarily have to do these exercises or chapters in order. A good way to dive in might be to take some time and go through the chapters, see what each involves, and then move through the material in the order you feel will work best for you. It's possible you might complete one section right away, put the book down for a while, and pick it back up later to work on a new section. This is your journey, so feel free to make it work for you. There is no right or wrong as far as which order you work because the exercises are standalone.

Over time and in your own way, through many subtle insights and shifts in your awareness, I hope you will feel lighter than before and experience greater peace in your life.

Keeping Track

During our time together, you're going to have many new insights, and you'll hopefully be able to release influences energetically and emotionally from your past while coming to a new understanding of your place in the world and how your actions can make a lasting and positive impact on the future members of your family and on humanity as a whole.

These insights will come to you from the depths of your soul, sometimes when you least expect them, and can often be so profound you will want to keep track of them. As with all my other books, I encourage you to record your progress by making notes in a journal of your choice. I'm a big believer in journals. If you're investing your precious time in reading this book, I assume that you recognize how important this kind of work can be. Ancestral Healing is not necessarily for everyone. It's a calling. With that kind of pull from your soul essence to assist and help your lineage, I can guarantee that at some point, you will have ideas and paradigm shifts in your thinking you will want to remember later. Insights and inner visions will pop up seemingly out of nowhere that can be so valuable to you, even if you cannot see exactly where they fit in at that moment. When you record these ideas for yourself, sometime down the road, you will likely be called to review them, and you never know what a difference these things can make for the future version of yourself. Think of your current self, the person reading these words right now, as a time traveler with insights and information that will benefit the future you, or even future generations of your family or of humanity. Don't let your personal inner wisdom slip through the cracks of your mind undocumented. Write it down.

The idea of keeping a journal seems quite overwhelming to some, so let me reassure you, it's super easy to do. By "journal," I'm talking about

- physical books with a cover and blank or lined pages,
- an app on your phone,
- a document on your tablet, or
- texting yourself a few thoughts.

The key is to find something you will actually use. There is no right or wrong as far as what kind of journal you choose. In each chapter, I've included suggested journal prompts to get you started. Use the questions I give you, or not, or write anything you believe will help you in the future.

Part One: Preparing for Ancestral Energy Healing

The book is divided into three parts. In the first part, I will review some basic considerations that will help you better prepare for Ancestral Energy Healing by describing and suggesting ways you can set up your environment in your home or office, where you can take guided journeys, and how to set up your very own Ancestral Healing altar to honor your lineage. You'll also journey into your own personal space within your mind's eye, where you will meet with your spirit guide, who will assist and accompany you on all the many experiences you will have in the book. You'll also meet with one of your own ancestors, who can serve as a second cosmic helper on the extraordinary adventure you're embarking on in Ancestral Energy Healing.

Part Two: Guided Journeys for Ancestral Energy Healing

In this part, I will guide you to dive deeper into several kinds of journeys, each designed to help you heal your ancestral lineage and heritage and emerge with greater self-understanding and peace. You will explore the following:

Forgiveness

Forgiveness is the initial door that opens to all kinds of healing. You will engage with some powerful exercises to release stagnant energies so you can open to further generational healing throughout the book.

Genealogical Regression

Genealogical Regression is the technique I developed over twenty years ago to help people create visual encounters and experiences with their ancestors. I will help you experience and discover the places that most need healing or that would most benefit your soul and your lineage. You'll learn how to identify challenging places within your ancestral lineage, send light to your ancestors, and feel the results within that will make a lasting impact on your inner peace while sharing your light with those who paved the way for you to be here.

Past-Life Regression

For over twenty years, I've helped people uncover and heal challenges through past-life regression. Although we are concerned with our families and ancestors in this book, it would be naïve for us not to consider that many of the people we interact with daily are people we've known in past lives. That is certainly and most definitely true of our parents, relatives, and ancestors. When you can explore the connections with family through the lens of past lives, you can come to an even greater understanding of the nuances, soul lessons, and soul gifts our family members bring to us over the course of time. This chapter will contain several exercises to help you explore your parents, your ancestors, and other relatives.

Rewriting Your History

Our ancestors endured great pain and difficulty. When you uncover such scenarios through the Genealogical Regression and past-life regression processes, you will have a chance to rewrite the most challenging chapters of your family's journey and experience a breaking of the difficult bonds and patterns that perpetuate inherited family trauma by releasing those unwanted influences and recreating your family story with the help of your ancestors. This is the first time these processes have appeared in print, but I assure you they are quite profound for healing.

Future Generational Healing

Once you learn to send light and healing to your ancestors, a shift occurs that begins to transform everyone in your family lineage—past, present, and future. In this section, you will discover how to consciously and effectively extend healing light and higher-vibrational frequencies to current living relatives as well as to future generations of your family.

The efforts you make in choosing to engage in these life-affirming practices have the potential to yield tremendous benefits for you on the spiritual path.

Part Three: Ancestral Energy Healing

In part three, I will introduce you to powerful energetic exercises you can do to heal the ancestral past within your own body that I collectively refer to as Ancestral Energy Healing. The term *energy healing* refers to the unseen part of yourself, the energetic aspect of you that exists beyond your physical self, the subtle energy that enlivens you. Thanks to new advancements in medicine, reputable organizations such as the National Institutes of Health now acknowledge the once fringe discipline of energy medicine and recognize the phenomenon that energy healers had pointed out for years—the subtle fields within and around the body can become blocked. Using healing methods including Reiki, Therapeutic Touch, and other techniques can help remove unwanted influences and blockages and restore well-being to the body, mind, and spirit.[9] I've discovered that each of us holds specific blocks that go well beyond our own past lives or current-life trauma and relate to things that happened to our ancestors from times long gone. Those subtle

---

9. Ross, "Energy Medicine," 2164956119831221.

influences linger in the subtle energy fields within and around your body. This phenomenon is largely outside of conscious awareness, yet by bringing attention to this area, tremendous healing can be achieved. In this book, you will learn easy-to-do exercises you can incorporate into your other spiritual practices to make a lasting impact on your energy field, and ultimately on your ancestors, by healing and releasing blocks related to things that happened within your lineage.

You will also learn how to acknowledge your familial energetic patterns within your body and do some deep healing and clearing that can leave you feeling more energized than ever before.

Summing Up

I believe wholeheartedly that countless individuals born at this time are spiritually called to engage in healing work on behalf of their ancestors. Is that you? Then please take my hand and join me on this epic journey to help heal the foundations of all it means to be human and pave the way for better times and brighter days for future generations.

Ancestral Energy Healing is a lifelong endeavor. Remember, the practices contained within these pages can be incorporated into your life at a pace of your own choosing and in alignment with your soul's purpose and higher calling to create greater peace, joy, and happiness for you, your forebears, and your entire ancestral lineage.

Part One

Preparing for Ancestral Energy Healing

To properly respect our ancestors and family members who have gone before us, it is important to create the proper space both in the outer three-dimensional world as well as within the inner world of your mind. This section will offer you a few ideas and suggestions to help you create the proper mindset and spaces to get the most out of the journeys in this book.

Beyond taking you through guided imagery journeys or suggesting ways you can set up your meditation room in your home or office, there are several other important considerations we must discuss up front to help you prepare for Ancestral Energy Healing. Creating the space to experience an open mind and heart is of paramount importance. In this first section, you will discover several ideas to create an experience that works best for you. As with any book or class, use this information for inspiration to create your own space in your own way.

There are several guided journey exercises you might want to record and play back to yourself that will begin in this section and continue throughout the remainder of the book. I will remind you when you may want to record something. These days, recording is so easy because you can find apps and download those onto your phone, tablet, or computer. The great thing about taking a little extra time to do that is you might want to repeat some of these exercises more than once, so if you record them, you will have them to use whenever you like. I will also recommend that you keep track of your progress in a journal so you can refer to those thoughts and ideas in the future.

CHAPTER ONE

Preparing Your Outer World

Throughout this book, you'll be honoring your ancestors. To experience the best outcomes, you will want to properly prepare both your outer and inner worlds. Most of us go through our daily lives as busy and incredibly distracted human beings, especially these days when the world puts so many demands on our time. In this chapter, I invite you to take some well-deserved me time to consider your surroundings and engage in simple but profound acts of self-love and care as you create a supportive and loving space to begin Ancestral Energy Healing.

Establishing Your Outer World

Before you can go within, you'll want to focus on your outer world and physical surroundings. To receive best results on any inner work, you will greatly benefit from spending a little time up front to create a physical space where you can feel supported and energized. Doing inner work and guided journeys requires concentration. Noises or feelings of physical discomfort can distract you and make things more difficult. Emotional issues may come up. By surrounding yourself with things you love that make you feel nurtured, you can go within surrounded by external feelings of comfort and security while minimizing anything that might stand in the way of getting the outcome you seek.

•• • ••
EXERCISE
Finding Your Comfortable Space

You may already have such a place in your home or office, and if so, that's great. If not, I recommend spending some time walking around your area and sensing the rooms where you feel most comfortable. Here is a quick exercise you can do.

Take a moment and walk around your home or office. Go room to room and as you do, ask yourself, "How do I feel here?" Make a mental note of the first thoughts that come.

Next, within the places you enjoy, sit down. Close your eyes and feel the energy at a deeper level. Again, notice how you feel as you sit quietly for a few minutes. If there is more than one place you tried, notice which area feels brighter and lighter to you. Also consider which space would provide the most privacy or quiet time. When you're ready, ask yourself, "Which space is best for me to use?" Notice the first thought that pops into your mind.

Make the decision to use this as your retreat area for this book and other spiritual practices. Try your chosen place for a period that feels right to you so you can see if the space works. If it does, wonderful, and if not, know that you can always change to another area later if you feel so guided.

•• • ••
JOURNAL PROMPT
Finding Your Comfortable Space

Take out your journal and consider the following.

1. How did you feel walking around your home or office searching for good energy?

2. Did you find areas you like more than others?

3. Which place did you choose and why? How did it make you feel?

As always, be open to more insights as your day progresses or notice if any thoughts emerge in the morning after a good night's rest. Writing these insights down can potentially help you in the future.

Decorating and Preparing Your Sacred Space

Once you find the space you love, you will want to make the energy as supportive as possible. To do that, I suggest doing a bit of decorating. This doesn't need to be anything elaborate or expensive, but taking the time to place things you love in your special space will help enhance the energy there and can help open you up to feel more secure and relaxed so you can go deeper into the many guided journeys you'll be doing later in the book.

Your sacred space is yours alone and only you can decide what you like. That task sounds easy enough, right? You would think so, but what I've found is that most of us are so busy in our lives, we often don't take time to really tune in to what we love and enjoy. You may find yourself taking care of others and going along with the group dynamic within the family or even with colleagues and friends. That is fine, of course, but here, for this space you're developing, I encourage you to take a little me time and find things that truly make your heart sing. A few places to look can include the following:

- **Seating**—Do you have a chair, sofa, or bench where you feel comfortable? Find something that supports your body so your muscles can relax. This will be particularly helpful during your guided imagery journeys later.

- **Scents**—Supporting yourself with the smells that make you feel happy and joyous or relaxed and calm can have a big impact on how you feel and how deeply you can dive into the depths of your subconscious mind and soul during journey work. Scents are powerful because they trigger emotion and memory in the brain. Finding those that support you can be helpful and make you feel calm. The fragrances you choose could come from essential oils such as lavender for relaxation. Scented candles, incense, or herb bundles made for burning can also put wonderful aromas into your space.

- **Lighting**—Consciously choosing your lighting can also help surround you with supportive energy. You might place dimmer switches into your lights so you can darken your space to prepare for guided journeys. You may prefer energizing lamps instead. Salt lamps cast healing glows around your space. Candles are a nice touch. If you're sensitive to smell, choose unscented. You could also light your space with artificial candles without having the worry of unattended flames.

- **Blankets and pillows**—Spiritual work goes deep and can often make dramatic changes in your body temperature. Keeping blankets around will help you stay warm. Pillows can support you both physically as well as emotionally and help you rest and relax.

- **Music**—Like scents, music goes straight into the brain and benefits you in numerous ways. Certain tones, such as binaural beats, actually attune your brain waves into calmer frequencies that can heal your body without any special effort on your part. Selecting music to play before you go into a guided journey or writing session in your journal can put you instantly into the proper frame of mind to get best results.

All the tools mentioned raise the vibrational frequencies of your sacred space and send unconscious intentions to the depths of your being that alert you that you're about to go on a spiritual journey. These are but a few of the endless possibilities you can use. Remember, this is your unique space, so anything you love will work. Also know that you might want to periodically change your surroundings to give your sacred space a refreshing update. It's all up to you. There's no right or wrong. Preparing your space in this way will yield powerful results for you as you prepare for your inner work. Enjoy the process of indulging yourself with things you love. You deserve the very best.

Creating Your Ancestral Altar

Once you've spent time creating a supportive space within your home or office and you've tried it out a few times, you can then dedicate a specific place within your area where you can honor your ancestors. Consciously paying tribute to your lineage in the physical world lets your ancestors know you're thinking about them and that you intend to create more love and peace within your family tree. That is an incredibly powerful message to convey to your lineage. Creating a place where you can focus on your ancestors can help you get the most out of the practices you will do throughout this book. Let's look at some basics.

Altar Considerations

Throughout the world since the earliest times in human history, people have honored their dead. The earliest known gravesites called the Levant Caves date back as far as 120,000 years,[10] and archaeological evidence proves that in the earliest times people honored their dead with grave goods and the intentional placement of bodies within early sites.[11] Through the centuries, worshipers created incredibly beautiful altars, shrines, and sacred spaces dedicated to their ancestors. Such altars can contain anything of value that ancestors would have enjoyed. For some people, it's one thing to make your own special place, but the idea of creating an altar for such an important purpose as ancestral appreciation can seem like an overwhelming task. Some questions may arise:

- *How can I possibly honor such important people?* The careful and loving intentions you use when creating your altar are appreciated by the ancestors. Your well wishes and the positive energy created by making the effort matter most.
- *Should this be a huge shrine?* Not unless you want it to be. In fact, most personal altars are quite small. Any space will work. The

---

10. Oldest, "8 of the Oldest-Known Human Graves in the World."

11. Henry, *Neanderthals in the Levant*, 25.

altar space is an area where you can use your conscious intent to humbly pay homage to your forebears. Small spaces such as bookshelves, tabletops, or windowsills can work. The intention is what matters.

- *Is the altar a permanent thing I need to make space for?* That is a personal question only you can answer. Are you someone who enjoys moving the furniture around a lot? If so, smaller portable altars may work best. That way, when doing housecleaning and dusting, you can easily remove and clean the altar and either put it back exactly the way you found it or make changes. It's all up to you. How comfortable you feel honoring your ancestors is what matters. The intention and the love you show are most important, so put what you love into a space you enjoy. Your loving energy will make your altar perfect for you.

Placing Your Ancestral Altar

Creating an altar or formal setting where you can focus your intentions is a wonderful place to begin. The process doesn't need to be even half as complicated as you may think. Your altar should be set up in a way you enjoy. A few ideas:

- **Bookshelf**—You can clear off a shelf where you can place special items that remind you of your relatives and ancestors.
- **Table**—The size of your table won't matter so long as you have room to put the things that are important to you.
- **Windowsill or seat**—Windows are great places for altars. The sun can shine in on the offerings, making them a calm and quiet place for reflection.
- **Outdoor garden**—Honoring ancestors in a garden is a beautiful gesture. Creating a memorial place where you can sit and reflect and simultaneously enjoy the healing powers of nature is wonderful. Within that wider garden, you may want to plant specific flowers or bushes that remind you of relatives—their favorites,

perhaps—or you may choose things that make you feel peaceful so you can bring forth that calm energy as you reflect and send healing light to your lineage.

The possibilities and options are as unique and unlimited as you are, so pick a place you find pleasing that you will be able to comfortably use as often as you'd like. The most important consideration is to put the altar in a place you enjoy where you will feel comfortable viewing and interacting with it. Set up a permanent place or a temporary place that you shift around with the seasons. It's all up to you and what makes you feel connected.

In addition to permanent places where you can work, you might want to make space for more flexible altars. For example, if you're someone who enjoys moving the furniture around a lot, you may want to create small altars that you can easily change around periodically. I've been known to take items with me on business trips and place tiny altars inside my hotel rooms. It's up to you how you feel most comfortable honoring your ancestors.

Tools and Items for Your Altar

Once the location is decided, you can begin placing items on or in your altar. Here are a few ideas to get you started:

- **Photos**—Gather up pictures of your family for your altar. This could include pictures of grandparents from times before your birth or photos of your extended family. Photos are only one aspect of your altar. You may not have any photos of any of your ancestors or family and have no idea who they were or what they looked like. That's okay too, but you can still connect with them on an energetic level. You can use other items to honor your ancestors whether you know anything about them or not.

- **Candles**—Memorials don't seem complete without some kind of candle to honor those who have gone before us. You can use real candles, or you may choose to use the LED ones that can remain lit safely while you're out or away from your altar. You could also try using both. Candles are a great symbol of remembrance for anyone you've loved and lost. Lighting a candle represents the eternal flame of the soul. Real flames are wonderful, but nowadays artificial LED candles are perfect to use for longer periods of time. If you like the idea of leaving candles burning, the best way to do that safely is with artificial candles.

• **Plants**—I mentioned creating a memorial garden for your ancestors. You could also place a plant on the shelf or table where your other items are located. If possible, you may want to select a plant that means something to you or reminds you of a particular person. When my paternal grandfather passed, I received a daylily from his funeral that I still care for to this day. The plant reminds me of him and makes me feel most connected. Again, you may not have such a plant or flower, but you could choose something you like and decide to dedicate that to your lineage.

• **Flowers**—Fresh flowers placed in a vase can provide another beautiful memorial to your forebears. Another point I must make is that we're not all green thumbs. If you don't enjoy tending plants, then perhaps that won't be the best choice for you. The items I mention here are but suggestions. Do what you think is best. One way around tending real plants could be to use silk flowers that don't ever fade. I have several in various altars in my space and they look lovely and only require occasional dusting.

• **Crystals**—Crystals can make an amazing addition to any kind of altar, ancestral or not. Each crystal has its own vibrational frequency and can immediately impact your space in a positive way. You could use amethyst for calming, rose quartz for love, or a clear quartz crystal. If there's a certain stone your family member liked, or a gem or mineral that specifically relates to your ancestral heritage, that can also make a great addition to your altar.

- **Artwork**—Did your ancestor paint or create other works of art? Handwoven lace, quilts, or other handiworks are wonderful keepsakes. Such priceless pieces are perfect for your altar.

- **Pottery**—Pottery or even small urns containing ashes can also be placed on your altar if you're so guided.

- **Jewelry and heirlooms**—Antique jewelry or other family treasures that you inherited and kept to commemorate your ancestors, such as silver or glassware, can be placed inside the altar. If you have furniture they owned, you could also set that up to use in the space you dedicated to your family.

- **Food**—In modern times, those who honor their ancestors often do so with food and drink offerings placed within the shrine or on the altar. You could use items of value to you or foods from the specific region where your family lived or items they loved during their lifetimes.

- **Herbal substances**—You can burn incense to honor your lineage. You might even find there are certain herbs that relate specifically to your family's cultural heritage, such as tobacco, which is considered sacred in certain Indigenous groups. If you feel guided and if that substance speaks to your soul and feels honoring, this is another option.

Any and all of these items can be placed in a memorial or within an altar whether they are family heirlooms or not. The main point is that you're using objects to remind you of the sacrifices of your ancestors and to pay homage to them. Everyone is different.

•• ● ••
EXERCISE
Creating an Ancestral Altar

The contents of your ancestral altar will be as varied as the people who live on this amazing planet. Do what you feel is best. Here's a quick exercise you can try to get you started.

Select a part of your home or office to dedicate to your ancestors. Prepare seating, a table, a shelf, or another area where you can place objects.

Once you've selected your space, go around your home or office and gather up any photos of your ancestors or earlier generations of your family that you enjoy. You may have very old photos, or you may only have more recent ones. Collect whatever you're guided to use.

Next, consider embellishing your ancestral area with candles, artifacts, heirlooms, and anything else that either belonged to a family member or that you could use to remind yourself of them. Take your time collecting these things for your new altar. Once you've gathered photos and your initial items, place them with love and purpose within the area you've chosen. Do your best, knowing you can always rearrange later.

When you feel that is complete, stand back and ask yourself, "What's missing?" Fill in the area with fresh or silk flowers, a plant, crystals, or anything else you believe will add to the ambiance of this special place.

At some point, finish with your altar and know all is well. Also realize that you can change it at any time by adding or removing things. If you're focusing on healing with one side of your family tree, for example, you may want to put those photos up only, then remove them later and work on the other side of the family. Use your intuition and do what you feel is best.

• • ● • •

JOURNAL PROMPT
Creating an Ancestral Altar

Take a moment, if you feel guided, to make a few notes in your journal about this process. Here are a few ideas to get you started.

1. What items did you collect for your altar?

2. Where did you place your altar?

3. Once you completed your altar, how did you feel there?

4. Will this be a place you can visit often for reflection?

Write down any other information you want to remember later. Handling heirlooms can bring up emotions about loved ones who passed on and so forth, so go gently, and if this process felt emotional to you, that's okay. You might want to make note of your feelings as well and notice how your feelings might evolve over time as you become more familiar with working with your altar.

Summing Up

Honoring and recognizing the significant role our ancestors played in our lives is a newly emerging trend within Western society. Thoughtfully engaging in the practice of placing special items in an altar or sacred space to reflect on your ancestors and seek their guidance is a perfect first step as you embark on your journey of Ancestral Energy Healing.

CHAPTER TWO
· · · · · · · · · · · · · · · ·
Establishing Your Inner World

Now that you've succeeded in setting up your personal space and creating an altar to honor your ancestors, you can move on to the important work of establishing a sacred space within the theater of your mind, in your inner world.

Consciously creating your inner world is one of the most beneficial and potentially life-changing exercises you can ever do for yourself. Consider this a gift of the spirit that you can carry with you always, regardless of your exterior circumstances. Beginning with the Emerald Tablet and the philosophies of Egyptian sage Hermes Trismegistus, spiritual sages and gurus throughout the ages have acknowledged the motto of "as above, so below" known as correspondence—the idea that the inner world pushes forth into conscious creation and three-dimensional reality.[12] That's why I will guide you in this chapter through the interior mindscape of your own inner world to help you create a place you love where you can feel totally accepted, loved, supported, and energized. From this launching pad, you can explore the many guided journeys and exercises involved in Ancestral Healing.

Once you set up your outer world by creating an altar and you have a place where you feel comforted to honor your ancestors, you can create

---

12. Ebeling, *Secret History of Hermes Trismegistus*, 50.

a special place in your inner world. There are a few steps to this process. First, you will find the doorway that leads to your inner sacred space, then you will go there, meet a personal guide, and enlist the help of an ancestral guide. Let's explore each of those steps now.

Finding Your Inner Sacred Space

In all our guided journeys in this book, you will walk through a doorway into your sacred space. Typically, when readers, clients, and students access this space, they discover it's the same place every single time. By returning to your special interior area every time you do guided imagery, you become more comfortable, and that sense of comfort will allow you to access the ancestors with increasing ease.

What this space looks or feels like is entirely up to you. Unlike the real world, this place can be filled with magical items that bring you tremendous comfort, and it can look or feel however you like, so long as it's comforting and relaxing and provides you with a deep sense of restoration and peace at the core of your being.

The first time you explore this place, you may not see many details, and that's okay. You can allow your space to reveal itself over time and become increasingly familiar to you with each progressive journey you take. Are you ready to explore this special place? For this journey and others like it, I suggest recording yourself on an app and playing this back so you can deepen your experience of visiting your sacred space. Let's begin.

•• • ••
EXERCISE
Finding Your Inner Sacred Space

Sit in a comfortable chair with your hands in your lap and feet flat on the floor. Close your eyes. Breathe. Take a deep, healing breath in through your nose, breathing in love and peace and light. Exhale any tensions and concerns. Continue to breathe, and as you do, you find yourself becoming more and more relaxed. Feel the breath going into your body. Imagine you are breathing in love, and joy, and relaxation, and peace, and you continue to exhale tensions and concerns. Very good. Continue to breathe and count as you do so, noticing that as you count and breathe, your state of inner peace is relaxing more and more. Ready?

Breathing in peace, joy, and love, and exhaling tensions. Continue to breathe. With each breath you take, you are becoming more and more relaxed. Find yourself breathing in peace, joy, and love as you release tensions and concerns.

Go ahead now and imagine a beautiful beam of pure white light coming down through the top of your head. Feel that light moving through your head and forehead, floating into your eyes, your nose, your mouth, and your jaw.

Continue to breathe as the light moves down, down, down, down, through your neck and shoulders, into your arms, your elbows, your wrists, your hands and fingertips.

Feel the light as it continues flowing down, down, down into your shoulders, your collarbone, your shoulder blades, and continues to flow down, down, down, into your heart center. Feel your heart's energy expand as the light continues to move down into your stomach, traveling down, down, down your spine and into your lungs, flowing down to the base of your spine. Continue to breathe as this loving light moves down, down, down, through the base of your spine, flowing into your legs—your thighs, your knees, your calves, your ankles and heels, and down into the soles of your feet and into your toes.

Imagine the light is getting stronger now as it moves from the crown of your head, all the way down through your body, through your spine, through your legs and down and out the soles of your feet. The light is becoming stronger now, so strong it begins to pour out of your heart center, creating a beautiful golden ball of light that surrounds you by about three feet in all directions. Imagine feeling yourself floating inside this peaceful golden ball of light. Know that within this golden ball of light, you are safe, secure, and totally carefree, and know that within the golden light, only that which is of your highest good can come through.

Imagine there's a doorway in front of you. You can see the door, feel the door, or just have an inner knowing the door is there. When you count back from three, you will walk through that door and go inside a beautiful room, a sacred space where you can feel totally relaxed, nurtured, and protected. Ready? Three, two, one; you're opening the door. Open the door now, and walk or float inside your beautiful room, a space you love and enjoy. Be there now and notice what's happening.

How do you feel in this special place?

What do you see there? Look around and notice all you can about your personal sacred space.

Take your time and bask in the feelings of peace and harmony as you take in all you can. Allow this place to fill your body with light and energy. Become fully refreshed and energized.

Pause here.

Take a deep breath in through your nose. Breathe in one, two, three, four, and exhale one, two, three, and four as you allow yourself to become completely relaxed inside your sacred space. Allow the supportive energies of your sacred space to move through every single cell of your being. As you do, breathe in the energy of joy, peace, and happiness as you inhale one, two, three, four, and exhale love and light, one, two, three, four. Very good.

Filled with peaceful light, feeling better than you did before, turn around and walk back through the door you came through and go out to where you began your journey. Be there now, back where you began. Close that door behind you and know you will be back there again very soon.

In a moment, when you count from five, you will come back into the room, feeling awake, refreshed, and better than you did before.

Five—grounded, centered, and balanced. Four—continuing to process this new energy in your dreams tonight so by tomorrow morning, you will be fully integrated into these new insights. Three—still surrounded by that beautiful golden ball of light, knowing that only that which is of your highest good can come through, you will find yourself driving carefully and being careful in all activities. Two—grounded, centered, and balanced, and one—you're back.

•• ● ••

JOURNAL PROMPT
Finding Your Inner Sacred Space

Take a moment to write down a few experiences. Here are some ideas to get you going.

1. How did you feel creating a state of relaxation and surrounding your body in light?
2. Could you sense the doorway? If so, how did it feel or what did it look like?
3. What did you find in your sacred space?
4. Describe what you saw, heard, or felt.
5. Had you been to this place before?

Record or make note of anything else that feels important. You will be returning to this special place throughout the entire book, so over time, your space will become very familiar to you.

Meeting Your Personal Guide

Have you ever been super down or overwhelmed, wondering what to do next, when suddenly you received a profound yet invisible touch on the shoulder, or a loosening of tensions in your back or neck followed by a deep and resonant feeling of peace that washed over you and seemingly came straight out of nowhere? I have, and I assure you, the feeling is not only surprising, but it happens to me so much that I began wondering who or what causes such beautiful feelings to occur. I've come to conclude that we are surrounded by loving helpful beings who guide and care for us throughout our life journeys. Everybody has these guides, including you, whether you've perceived their presence yet or not.

To fully engage in Ancestral Energy Healing, you'll want to connect with a source of support that you can lean on during these exercises. For that reason, you will take a journey to connect you with a guide who will accompany you throughout the remainder of this book and perhaps beyond this work. You may already have a spiritual practice that incorporates working with a loving guide, angel, or group of spiritual beings or counselors. If so, that's awesome. If not, this journey will help you establish this important helper. Your Ancestral Healing guide may appear to you as any number of incarnations:

- **Angel**—You may encounter what could be described as a guardian angel who will meet you in your space.
- **Archangel**—Archangels such as Michael, Uriel, Raphael, and others are quite common and popular guides for many people.
- **Ball of light**—Some meet with pure consciousness in the shape of a ball.
- **Deceased friend or relative**—Meeting loved ones who have crossed over is a bit less common in this space, but certainly possible. Your loved one may wish to assist you with your journey from the other side.
- **Light being**—Your special guide may have a human shape but appear as pure love, light, and consciousness. This is a fairly common experience for many seekers. Most of the time these beings are faceless and feel like bright balls of unconditional love.
- **Animals in spirit**—Animal guides are powerful assistants for some and can possibly be the energy that appears for you during this process.

Regardless of what kind of guide you have, the guide will be your constant companion throughout your Ancestral Energy Healing journey.

They will be someone who has known you and your soul since the beginning of time. They love you unconditionally, and because they theoretically know you better than you know yourself, they provide an invaluable resource for you as you go through the Ancestral Healing process.

However your special guide shows up for you, regardless of what form they take, is perfect. There's no right or wrong. They will be right by your side and are meant to help you with the journeys ahead. For simplicity's sake with so many options, I will be referring to your special someone as your "guide." Meeting them and knowing them will help enable you to share that same guidance, unconditional love, and wisdom with your own ancestors in the chapter on Genealogical Regression.

Even if you already have a guide you've been working with for years, keep an open mind. You never know who will show up and it may be someone new. I encourage you to take the journey with an open heart because you never know what can unfold. In my books and classes, students and readers typically report that there is one special guide who works with them throughout a specific project. In Ancestral Energy Healing, there may be a guide who will appear who you have known about for years but may not have worked with before. Anything's possible.

There is still another possibility that a brand-new guide wants to introduce themselves to you, someone who is tasked with the assignment of helping you with Ancestral Energy Healing and resolving ancestral trauma within your soul's journey. Normally once this guide is introduced, they will stay right by your side throughout the remainder of the book. Maybe, maybe not, but be prepared and expect the unexpected and wonderful blessings to emerge. Are you ready to meet your guide? This is another exercise that will likely be easier to do if you find an app and record and play the journey back to yourself.

•• • ••
EXERCISE
Meeting Your Personal Guide

Retreat to your personal sacred space and prepare yourself for comfort. Close your eyes, breathe, and relax. Continue to breathe in peace, joy, and love as you release tensions and concerns.

Go ahead now and imagine a beautiful beam of pure white light coming down through the top of your head. Feel that light moving through your head and forehead, floating into your eyes, your nose, your mouth, and your jaw.

Continue to breathe as the light moves down, down, down, down, through your neck and shoulders, into your arms, your elbows, your wrists, your hands and fingertips.

Feel the light as it continues flowing down, down, down into your shoulders, your collarbone, your shoulder blades, and continues to flow down, down, down, into your heart center. Feel your heart's energy expand as the light continues to move down into your stomach, traveling down, down, down your spine and into your lungs, flowing down to the base of your spine. Continue to breathe as this loving light moves down, down, down, through the base of your spine, flowing into your legs—your thighs, your knees, your calves, your ankles and heels, and down into the soles of your feet and into your toes.

Imagine the light is getting stronger now as it moves from the crown of your head, all the way down and out the soles of your feet. The light is becoming stronger now, so strong it begins to pour out of your heart center, creating a beautiful golden ball of light that surrounds you by about three feet in all directions. Imagine feeling yourself floating inside this peaceful golden ball of light. Know that within this golden ball of light, you are safe, secure, and totally carefree, and know that within the golden light, only that which is of your highest good can come through.

Imagine there's a doorway in front of you. You can see the door, feel the door, or just have an inner knowing the door is there. When you count back from three, you will walk through that door and go inside your sacred space where you can feel totally relaxed, nurtured, and protected. Ready? Three, two, one; you're opening the door. Open the door now, and walk or float inside your beautiful room, a space that you love and enjoy. Be there now and notice what's happening.

Look around and connect with the feelings of peace and harmony as you take in all you can. Allow this place to fill your body with light and energy. Become fully refreshed and energized.

Pause here.

Imagine a beautiful angel, spirit guide, or being of light is floating down to join you now. Feel them land right next to you. Notice what you can about them. Are they an angel, a light being, or a spirit guide? Have you seen them before?

Know now that this loving presence with you is your guide who has been with your soul since the beginning of time. They love you unconditionally. Feel the love they have for you now. Receive that and know you are so very, very loved.

Pause here.

Understand that this loving guide knows every single thing there is to know about you and your soul and your soul's journey. They know you better than you know yourself and they love you. Bask in that love now, knowing that through them, you have a trusted guide and friend who will look out for you and your best interests. Feel that love now.

Pause here.

Know that you will be working with your guide extensively throughout this book and beyond. Take a moment to thank them for joining you today. For now, say goodbye and imagine your guide is floating up and away, going back to where they came from. Know they will see you again very soon.

Take your time and bask in the feelings of peace and harmony as you take in all you can. Allow this place to fill your body with light and energy. Become fully refreshed and energized.

Pause here.

Take a deep breath in through your nose. Breathe in one, two, three, four, and exhale one, two, three, and four as you allow yourself to become completely relaxed inside your sacred space. Allow the supportive energies of your sacred space to move through every single cell of your being. As you do, breathe in the energy of joy, peace, and happiness as you inhale one, two, three, four, and exhale love and light, one, two, three, four. Very good.

Filled with peaceful light, feeling better than you did before, go ahead and turn around now and walk back through the door that you came through and go back out to where you began your journey. Be there now, back where you began. Close that door behind you and know you will be back there again very soon.

In a moment, when you count from five, you will come back into the room, feeling awake, refreshed, and better than you did before.

Five—grounded, centered, and balanced. Four—continuing to process this new energy in your dreams tonight so by tomorrow morning, you will be fully integrated into these new insights. Three—still surrounded by that beautiful golden ball of light, knowing that only that which is of your highest good can come through, you will find yourself driving carefully and being careful in all activities. Two—grounded, centered, and balanced, and one—you're back.

•• ● ••

JOURNAL PROMPT
Meeting Your Personal Guide

Take some time to consider the following and make some notes.

1. How did you feel returning to your sacred space?

2. Did you experience the loving energy of your guide?

3. Describe your guide visually or through your inner thoughts or feelings about them.

4. How did it feel to receive unconditional love and understanding from your guide?

5. Record any other thoughts or ideas that emerge.

Please remember you are on a journey and not at a destination. What you did today was transformative and helpful. Be open to the thoughts that may pop in over the coming days and weeks or even in your dreams. Be sure to continue your notes about anything you may find helpful. Know you will learn much more about your guide as you go through this book. Even if you didn't see or feel much today, that's okay. Allow the information to unfold over time.

Remember that the guide you met today could be any number of iterations. You may have met an angel, a light being, or even an ancestor. With most of my students, readers, and clients, only one guide shows up, but it's also possible that two may appear. You might even find that both guides accompany you on all the journeys in this book, or certain guides might be with you for some journeys and not others. If that's the case, remain open to what you experience by holding the space for whichever guide or guides appear, and know you're receiving exactly what you need for your journeys.

Meeting Your Ancestral Guide

Many of the world's traditions recognize and understand that our ancestors deserve our respect and should be celebrated. Many recognize their ancestors as guides who offer wise counsel regarding how to proceed with any number of earthly duties and activities. Once we begin the journey of truly helping our ancestors, we open the door of communication so that our ancestors hear our call, thank us for our help, and gladly reciprocate by sharing their light with us after we simply acknowledge their presence and appreciate their sacrifices.

•• ● ••
EXERCISE
Meeting Your Ancestral Guide

Because you're doing the important and special work of Ancestral Energy Healing, it is quite possible that an ancestral guide could appear to assist you. This may be someone who lived hundreds of years ago who wishes to play an important role in your healing journey. They may wish to gift you with specific knowledge, or they may accompany you and the guide you met earlier throughout this entire process of Ancestral Energy Healing to add another layer of wisdom to your path. Record the journey for best results.

Retreat to your comfortable chair. Sit with your hands in your lap and feet flat on the floor. Close your eyes. Breathe. Take a deep, healing breath in through your nose, breathing in love and peace and light. Exhale any tensions and concerns. With each breath you take, you are becoming more and more relaxed. Find yourself breathing in peace, joy, and love as you release tensions and concerns.

Go ahead now and imagine a beautiful beam of pure white light coming down through the top of your head. Feel that light moving through your head and forehead, floating into your eyes, your nose, your mouth, and your jaw, moving down, down, down, through your neck and shoulders, into your arms, your elbows, your wrists, your hands and fingertips.

Feel the light flowing down, down, down into your shoulders, your collarbone, your shoulder blades, and continuing to flow down, down, down, into your heart center. Feel your heart energy expand as the light continues to move down into your stomach, traveling down, down, down your spine and into your lungs, flowing down to the base of your spine, moving into your legs—your thighs, your knees, your calves, your ankles and heels, and down into the soles of your feet and into your toes.

Imagine the light pours out of your heart center, creating a beautiful golden ball of light that surrounds you by about three feet in all directions. Know that within the golden light, only that which is of your highest good can come through.

Notice your doorway in front of you. When you count back from three, you will walk through that door and float into your beautiful room. Allow this place to fill your body with light and energy. Become fully refreshed and energized.

Pause here.

As you continue to enjoy your sacred space, imagine your loving guide is floating down to join you now. Take a moment and let your guide know that today you would like to meet with an ancestral guide. This may be an ancestor who wishes to join you on many journeys, or it may be an ancestor who would like to share important information with you today. Take your time to speak with your guide about this now.

Pause here.

Very good. Notice now there's a doorway on the other side of your sacred space. That door is opening now, and here comes your ancestor. Imagine seeing, feeling, or just knowing your ancestor is with you now. They approach you and you notice how happy they are to see you. Take your time while your ancestor introduces themselves to you.

Pause here.

Ask your ancestor for any wisdom or helpful information they would like to share with you that can help you on your path. Ask questions and gain clarity on what they're sharing.

Pause here.

When you're ready, thank your ancestor for being with you today. Notice now they are walking or floating back through the door they came through. Turn to your other guide and speak to them about what you discovered and receive any other insights.

Pause here.

Thank your guide for assisting you today as they say goodbye and float away. Turn around and go back out to where you began your journey, closing your door behind you.

You're back to where you began. When you count back from five, you will return, feeling awake, refreshed, and better than ever before.

Five—you're grounded, centered, and balanced. Four—processing this information in your dreams tonight, so by tomorrow, you'll be fully integrated into this new awareness. Three—driving safely and being safe in every activity. Two—grounded, centered, and balanced, and one—you're back.

How did that go?

•• ● ••

JOURNAL PROMPT
Meeting Your Ancestral Guide

Take a moment to reflect on what you learned. Here are a couple of suggested questions you can answer.

1. Did you meet an ancestor today? If so, who?
2. What information did they share to help you with your life?
3. Did you sense they will return to assist with other journeys, or did they only visit to share specific details with you?

If you could not perceive an ancestor, that's okay. Keep working and know, over time, information will emerge. When you take this journey again later, you can meet with new ancestors or meet the one who visited you today again to receive more valuable information.

Summing Up

Establishing an inner space to do your Ancestral Healing is of paramount importance. Consider your inner world a sanctuary where you can go anytime you need to retreat from the stresses and pressures of daily life to gain rejuvenation and peace. Likewise, you can use this place anytime in the future to go and gain new perspectives and helpful insights that can enhance the quality of your life from here on out.

Part Two

Guided Imagery
for Ancestral Energy Healing

Now that you've established a set place where you can feel comfortable doing your spiritual work and you've visited your inner sanctuary and met with trusted helpers and guides, this next section will begin the deeper inner work of guided imagery.

I cannot stress enough the importance of taking this information at your own pace. If you feel comfortable doing these exercises, that's wonderful, but if not, that's good too. Do them in your time, in your way, and be gentle with yourself. Ancestral Energy Healing is difficult. It takes incredible courage and inner strength to work through the multilayered situations experienced by your forebears. Know that just reading over an exercise, even if you don't feel up to doing it yet, begins to open the door to your inner world to contemplate the healing that's being suggested. Every little bit helps.

I also must emphasize how important your imagination is in creating the life you truly want to live. Everything that appears in our outer world must first originate with a thought. When you go into your inner sanctuary within your mind and you feel loved and supported by guides and angels who love you unconditionally and have your best interests in mind, you can feel secure enough to go into the deeper work of self-healing and transformation.

By working on yourself and gaining new perspectives about your past, doors open for you to go beyond the self and extend that healing light out to your ancestors in the past and ultimately to those generations who have yet to be born.

Every person alive has a chance during this important and unique time in history to raise frequencies and transform humanity for the better. These exercises in this section of the book will help you open those doors gently, yet powerfully. Remember that you are in charge of how your journey unfolds, so feel free to do the processes in order or only complete the ones you feel guided to do at the moment. Whatever you decide is perfect.

CHAPTER THREE
. . . .
Forgiveness—Doorway to Healing

Through the years, I've noticed one huge roadblock that all people need to overcome to access past lives or to engage in the deeper work of Ancestral Energy Healing: forgiveness. There is simply nothing as difficult to do in this life, or any former incarnation, than to forgive those who have wronged us. That concept is particularly tough when individuals are faced with unspeakable traumas, abuse, and crimes against them. How does one move forward in trying to forgive an abuser, for example? Child abuse survivors are a class of individuals who have huge mountains to climb when it comes to finding peace with their past. Forgiveness is a multilayered journey and simply cannot be done in one sitting. How we would all love to wave our magical wands and make certain things vanish from our lives, and yet, that doesn't happen. All one can expect from forgiveness is to peel off layer upon layer of pain. Slowly, over time, relief begins to happen. How long that might take is anybody's guess. Everyone is different. You may find this is one chapter you simply cannot do right now, and if not, that's okay.

On the flip side, we know human beings inherit family trauma, as shown by many recent studies. Despite that, I find myself asking why we only focus on the negative. Why can't we come to another realization that must be true—if we pick up trauma from ancestors, do we also pick up blessings? Of course! Where do you think you get that special affinity for the piano even though you never had one? Why do you love to paint? Scientists are studying this right now. One study sought to see if elite athletes inherit their talents from their forebears, and while the study suggested that is indeed the case, the findings were still inconclusive for now.[13] I still believe you pick up your gifts, talents, interests, and love of certain things from your family. As time goes on and science continues to advance, humanity will eventually gain further clarity about these connections.

Although your ancestors endured great traumas, Ancestral Energy Healing can be used for other purposes than merely to heal those unimaginable hardships. You can also expand your consciousness to include the numerous positive influences, gifts, and talents your ancestors passed down to you. To begin to engage with this important paradigm shift where Ancestral Energy Healing is concerned, we need to consider a few crucially important things:

- **Grace**—Recognizing people are likely doing the best they can most of the time.
- **Compassion**—Feeling merciful about the pain and suffering of others.
- **Empathy**—Putting yourself in other people's shoes.
- **Forgiveness**—Releasing resentments over past transgressions, no matter how painful, to release stuck energy that holds you back.

Let's take a closer look at each.

Grace

What does *grace* imply? That we acknowledge every single one of us, no matter how great our merits, is a human being. Yes, we are spiritual beings having a human experience. I know that too, but indulge me for a moment here. We are also in these bodies at this time in history to be here, to be embodied in a human form. As such, our broader and more

---

13. Pickering, "Can Genetic Testing Identify Talent for Sport?" 12.972.

widely expansive scope of how the universe and Source energy should work is a bit limited. We simply cannot be in a body and always understand the complexities and higher ideals of the spiritual nature of ourselves. That's why we came here—to evolve, grow, and learn in order to hopefully be better and more enlightened than when we showed up here. As such, it is a wonderful policy to extend this grace or understanding about the limited nature of our physical selves not only to ourselves in the form of self-love and self-acceptance, but to other humans who share our planet with us at this time in history. We should also extend that grace to our forebears, our lineage, and our ancestors. We do not always know what they faced. They may not have made the best decisions because of the hardships they endured and the pressures of trying to survive. Most people do the best they can with their circumstances. Can you envision your ancestors as trying their best to survive hardships brought on by the outer world?

Do people from all these groups bother us, make us angry, or hurt our feelings and do things that are completely unacceptable at times? Things that are theoretically unforgivable? Yes, of course they do. Extending grace is not saying that any unwanted or horrific behaviors are condoned, nor should they be, but for you and I to heal ourselves, we must be able to release unwanted influences surrounding any others who have harmed us, and at times, the ones who seem to hurt us the most are our family members.

Compassion

Why do people do what they do? If someone wrongs you and is a horrible person, is it possible that somewhere in their current lifetime someone treated them so badly that they do not know how to behave? That is the spirit of finding compassion we will work from in this Ancestral Energy Healing process. All people struggle with various aspects of life. Showing compassion toward their plight assists us on the spiritual path. Our ancestors endured so much pain and struggle; finding compassion is a key to healing the past.

Empathy

Putting yourself in another's place is a high ideal. We may not like the actions people take, but presuming that, despite outward appearances, most people are simply doing the best they can allows us to empathize with them and opens us up to more expansive energy. The pressures your ancestors braved to simply stay alive are likely unimaginable. Empathy helps us appreciate those struggles, and while we don't want to lose ourselves in grieving what might have occurred in the past, showing that empathy toward their plight produces tremendous healing.

Forgiveness

Forgiveness is perhaps the most challenging but life-affirming consideration of them all. Obviously, we have all had the idea of forgiveness brought up to us, and how it's imperative to our own happiness. At times when we hear things too much, we tend to turn off those messages and ignore them altogether. That said, it's true. Forgiving others is the absolute key to your happiness. I said *your* happiness, not theirs. That's important. It does not matter whether the person you are forgiving deserves it or if you're ever even able to express such a sentiment to them in person. Holding on to that resentment and old stagnant energy is damaging you. For all you know, they haven't thought about you or considered you in years, and yet you may be holding on to something old and toxic. When we do the healing processes in the Genealogical Regression chapter and beyond, one of the biggies is to meet the parents or other family members in a state of what I like to call soul essence or Higher Self. This means that they are not the person who wronged you. They are not the person who hurt you unimaginably. You will not be engaging with the real-life person who became your parent, even if you have an awesome relationship with them. You will engage with their soul. At the soul level, even the most unenlightened person can become more tolerable. For some, depending on the hurt, getting to a place to even be able to converse with this parent still may take a while. That's where baby steps are perfect. If you are truly committed to the work of Ancestral Healing (and yes, it is work), then you must extend the grace to yourself to allow your forgiveness journey to be what it can be and to take your time working through tough feelings until you can reach a state of neutrality. If you aren't there yet and cannot forgive, that is okay too. The qualities of grace and compassion must be extended to you first and foremost.

Forgiving Your Parents

Forgiveness is one of, if not *the*, biggest obstacle seekers face when doing any kind of healing work, whether you're engaging in Ancestral Healing, a Genealogical Regression, or a past-life regression. It's hard to dig into the deeper family or soul issues if you cannot get past the pains of your present life. I discovered this early in my career when working with my clients. When people sought past-life regressions from me, I realized on an intuitive level that they would have a very difficult time accessing those spaces until they could do current-life healing. That could be relating to issues with a spouse, sibling, or friend, but most of the time, the issues were with the client's parents.

Defining the Term "Parent"

Speaking of parents, one important topic we need to cover now is what the term *parent* really means. *Parent* means different things to different people. You may know your birth parents and perhaps you were raised by them, but that's not the case for everyone. There are lots of possibilities for who you may engage with as a parent within Ancestral Healing. Whether someone is your blood relative or not makes no difference. The people who come into your life do so for a reason. There is a soul connection there and that exists within several different models of parents:

- **Birth parents**—Whether you know your birth parents or not, they are an important consideration in Ancestral Healing. Those who are adopted can still encounter the energy and soul essences of their birth parents to do deep and important Ancestral Healing work.

- **Adoptive parents**—There is perhaps no greater love a parent can show to someone than to choose to adopt. The soul connection you share with adoptive parents is profound.

- **Foster parents**—Likewise, those who foster children provide caregiving that is essential to many. If you found yourself in a foster situation, there is a soul connection there that can be explored.

- **Grandparents**—Grandparents play an important role for many people and often become the main parental figure in people's lives.

- **Mentors**—At different times on the life path, you may have encountered an important mentor, teacher, or other adult who nurtured and supported you.

- **Institutional caregivers**—Kind souls from adoption agencies or other care facilities you experienced growing up can also be sources of soul connections.

I've suggested a few here, but you may have something different in your life other than what I described. Just know that *parent* can mean anyone who became part of your development story when you were growing up.

While ideally all your relationships were positive, again, that is not realistic for everyone, and as such, these figures can sometimes become the source of angst and focal points of much-needed forgiveness to enable you to move forward in life in the best way possible.

The repeated issues I saw with so many people regarding the need to forgive a parental figure were aided repeatedly by the conversations people had in their inner worlds with their parents, family members, friends, or other loved ones who wronged them. Going into your sacred space and engaging in conversations where you're able to express hurt feelings or other incidents that perhaps you've never had a chance to express in the "real world" can be incredibly powerful. Doing these processes proved extremely transformational to my past clients and helped them go into deeper places within their minds. I can say with 100 percent certainty that forgiveness is the single biggest key to transformation there is. Once you master that one, the sky's the limit on what you can accomplish.

Higher Selves of Parents

Once you decide which parental figure to work with, I must also mention another important consideration. During the Genealogical Regression that you will do later in the book, you will go on a guided journey into a sacred space and meet with your mom's and dad's *Higher Selves.* What does that mean? Instead of encountering your parents as the flawed three-dimensional physical human beings they are or were in real waking life, you will instead meet with their soul essences and appeal to their more evolved and spiritual aspects. Meeting them at the level of the Higher Self is critical for success. We all know that our family relationships are challenging at best. Understanding the meeting as spiritual is important because often our parents have said or done things that may be completely unacceptable or unforgivable. When that happens, it would be tough, if not impossible, to carry on a conversation with them. Understanding that you are not meeting with who they are in the outer world can help you suspend any resentments or hurt feelings caused by their real-world actions. Meeting them at the soul level that is totally spiritual in nature and completely beyond anything they may have done or said in waking life can help you receive the necessary apologies or unconditional love you may not have ever received in waking life. This step away from the real-life people you encountered in your past can give you the strength to move past those real-life hurts in order to release unwanted influences that keep you from having a peaceful life. Once you get past the present life and release some of the more challenging energies, you will free yourself to release whatever happened in the past and move beyond that to encounter and send healing light to the prior generations of your family.

Parents You Know or Strangers

Because your parent could be a birth parent, adoptive or foster parent, mentor, grandparent, or any other possibility, another reason for meeting parents at the level of the Higher Self is the fact that you may or may not know your parents in real life. Perhaps you were adopted and never knew your birth family. Maybe your parents passed away and your grandparents raised you. If you only focus on whatever happened to you in real life, then that would make it impossible to do healing with them or encounter them in any meaningful way.

All real healing begins in the imagination, in that inner world you explored in the prior chapter. By engaging with parents at the soul level within your safe and sacred inner world, you can have visionary encounters with those who are no longer around or who you never met, and these experiences can make lasting and profound impacts on your life even if you never met these parents before. The realm of the spirit knows no boundaries, and as you explore this boundless realm, you can receive the light and love you need for greater peace and happiness in your life. When you're able to heal and shift unwanted influences in your inner world, your outer world and current-life experience become instantly transformed and lighter.

Apologies, Forgiveness, and Unconditional Love

First up, you'll take a guided journey to meet with the parent figure of your choice to experience a conversation that can result in healing and forgiveness. Remember that the parent figure could be anyone, including a foster parent, an aunt, an uncle, a grandparent. Everybody is different, so think about the parental figures who influenced you in the past. Within the security and comfort of your sacred space, you can receive unconditional love that you may not have experienced from these parental figures before in real life. By going through this shorter journey first, you will hopefully experience more extensive healing later.

Building on what you already did in the last chapter, you will go back into your sacred space where you will connect with the supportive energy of your main guide who will help you with insights and support you along the way. While there, you will meet your parent and have a heartfelt conversation.

Before you begin, you may want to decide in advance if you want to meet with the Higher Self of your mom, dad, or another parent figure. If you prefer, you could also just allow your highest good to come through and see which parent shows up. If you leave your options open and your dad comes through, for example, you can always take the journey again later to meet with your mom. Another option is to consider doing this journey with any of the different parental figures you've had in your life.

•• ● ••
EXERCISE
Apologies, Forgiveness, and Unconditional Love

Forgiveness may be the outcome, or you may be someone who has a wonderful relationship with your parent figure. If that's the case, use this journey to feel grateful for your parent and to connect with their unconditional love and support. Know that the relationship will only expand and become enhanced through contact with their Higher Self. Always keep in mind that during your journey, the highest good comes through and things emerge in the best time for all concerned. Ready? Let's begin.

Sit in a comfortable chair with your hands in your lap and feet flat on the floor. Close your eyes. Breathe. Take a deep, healing breath in through your nose, breathing in love and peace and light. Exhale any tensions and concerns. Continue to breathe, and as you do, you find yourself becoming more and more relaxed. Feel the breath going into your body. Imagine you are breathing in love, and joy, and relaxation, and peace, and you continue to exhale tensions and concerns. Very good. Continue to breathe and count as you do so, noticing that as you count and breathe, your state of inner peace is relaxing more and more. Ready?

Breathing in peace, joy, and love and exhaling tensions. Continue to breathe. With each breath you take, you are becoming more and more relaxed. Find yourself breathing in peace, joy, and love as you release tensions and concerns.

Go ahead now and imagine a beautiful beam of pure white light coming down through the top of your head. Feel that light moving through your entire body, flowing all the way through your arms and legs and down and out the soles of your feet.

The loving light pours from your heart center and surrounds you by about three feet in all directions. Within this supportive golden light, only your highest good can come through.

When you count back from three, you will walk through the door and go inside your sacred space. Ready? Three, two, one; you're opening the door. Open the door now.

Notice your loving guide is floating down to join you now. Feel them land right next to you. Feel the immense unconditional love they have for you. Know they are here to support you in this journey.

Take a moment to discuss your intentions for today. Let your guide know that you would like to meet with one of your parents to have an important conversation of forgiveness and healing.

Pause here.

Once you finish speaking with your guide, notice there's a door on the other side of your sacred space and that door is opening now, and here comes one of your parents. Notice this person now. Who is this? Note the first thought that comes into your mind. Very good.

Know that this is their Higher Self, the highest aspect of their soul. Feel the essence of their soul now and know this is beyond the person you may know in life. Notice at this level, your parent figure is happy, healthy, and so very glad to see you.

Let your parent know that you're here today to begin the healing process between the two of you. Take your time to express to them anything you need to say today. This may be love and gratitude, or it may be time now for you to let them know about anything that hurt you through the years that you would like to address with them. Take your time and imagine that at the Higher Self level, your parent figure is open, receptive, and listening to you express your needs and concerns.

Pause here.

When you're ready, allow them to respond sincerely to you. Imagine that at the Higher Self level, they can apologize sincerely for anything they may have done through the years to hurt you. Imagine they are expressing their deepest regrets and letting you know they are truly sorry and that they were simply doing the best they knew how to do at the time. Take your time again and have this important conversation.

Pause here.

If possible, imagine you can accept this apology. Feel the weight of former resentments lifting from your body and evaporating as you open to the healing light of forgiveness. If you find you cannot forgive, could you find a bit of room to release tension around the issue? If so, imagine you could feel a bit better about the situation than you did before. Take a moment as you process this feeling of expanded energy.

Pause here.

Imagine now that your parent figure lets you know how much they love you. This love is coming to you from their soul to yours. As such, this is unconditional love. Perhaps they have never expressed this to you in the outer world, but know now, in this place, your parent has a deep desire to express their love for you. Let them tell you, show you, they may want to hug you. Take your time as they express their unconditional love, and again, even if this is nothing you have ever experienced with them before, know this is sincere and receive that conversation and unconditional love now.

Pause here.

Imagine as you receive this, your entire being is filled with this lightness and healing as you understand that at the soul level, your parent figure loves you. Feel and allow that knowing to come into every single cell in your being.

Pause here.

When you're ready, you may choose to say anything else to them, including sharing your love with them as well, or not. Take a moment in whatever way you choose to respond to this unconditional love you've received.

Pause here.

When you're ready, imagine your parent can thank you for assisting with this healing today. They truly appreciate you hearing them out and sharing this conversation and energy exchange. They want to remind you that regardless of what happened in the past, you are loved.

Pause here.

When you're ready, say goodbye for now, knowing you will be seeing them again very soon. Imagine they can walk or float back through the door they came through, closing that door behind them. Turn your attention back to your guide. Take a moment to allow your guide to send you unconditional love, support, and feedback or counsel about the conversation you just shared with your parent's Higher Self.

Pause here.

Thank your guide for their loving support. Say goodbye for now and watch while they float back to where they came from.

Take a deep breath in through your nose. Breathe in one, two, three, four, and exhale one, two, three, and four as you allow yourself to become completely relaxed inside your sacred space. Allow the supportive energies of your sacred space to move through every single cell of your being. As you do, breathe in the energy of joy, peace, and happiness as you inhale one, two, three, four, and exhale love and light, one, two, three, four. Very good.

Filled with peaceful light, feeling better than you did before, turn around now and walk back through the door to where you began your journey. Be there now, back where you began. Close that door behind you and know you will be back there again very soon.

In a moment, when you count from five, you will come back into the room, feeling awake, refreshed, and better than you did before.

Five—grounded, centered, and balanced. Four—continuing to process this new energy in your dreams tonight so by tomorrow morning, you will be fully integrated into these new insights. Three—still surrounded by that beautiful golden ball of light, knowing that only that which is of your highest good can come through, you will find yourself driving carefully and being careful in all activities. Two—grounded, centered, and balanced, and one—you're back.

•• ● ••

JOURNAL PROMPT
Apologies, Forgiveness, and Unconditional Love

Take a moment to reflect on all you received on this journey. Here are a few ideas for what you may want to write down.

1. Which person visited with you today?
2. Did you receive an apology from them?
3. What other things were discussed?
4. How did it feel to receive their love?
5. What insights did you receive to help you on your path in the future?

This work may have been incredibly emotional for you. You might need time to process what you received. Allow yourself the space to do so gently. You may need to take a break or record thoughts and insights in your journal over a period of time in order to process what happened.

When you feel up to it, you could also repeat this process with a different person you want to work on. For example, if your mom showed up today, you can do the journey again with your dad or someone else whenever you feel guided and ready to do so. You may find you want to take this journey more than once with each parent, depending on the specific situation and need for healing. Again, all of that should be done if and when you're ready to do so.

Keep in mind that healing and forgiving is a journey, not a destination. It takes time. If you found that this person was impossible to forgive, that's okay. Even if you can't forgive, then perhaps you were able to bring a bit more light into the heavy energy of the situation. Maybe not. Know that whatever you feel is okay. If you're guided, you can always keep trying down the road. You may be able to work on this situation over time and experience more healing.

Forgiving Beyond the Family

While you're in this forgiving space, an important consideration is the fact that any challenges you have with anyone can affect your ability to engage in deeper levels of inner peace or Ancestral Healing. Perhaps you did that last journey, for example, and found your parents were amazing and no healing was needed. If that's the case, awesome!

There is not a soul alive, however, who doesn't have a challenge with some member of the human species. That's just part of life. Next, I offer you more forgiveness journeys to lighten your soul. There are three areas where forgiveness can offer unparalleled transformation in your life:

- **Forgiveness from others**—There's not a soul alive who hasn't inadvertently wronged someone. By recalling those times and experiencing mutual grace, healing begins, and you open yourself to other forms of forgiveness.

- **Forgiving others**—The big reason why you and I are here in the first place is to release stuck energy of the past. A great place to work on that is through the heartfelt and sincere forgiveness of other people.

- **Forgiving yourself**—Many people are first to offer others the benefit of the doubt while being incredibly hard on themselves.

This is part of human nature. In this section, you will learn how to create more love of self by letting yourself off the hook and forgiving your past.

In the following sections, you will explore each of these areas further.

Forgiveness from Others

The first of our three forgiveness journeys involves your journey to asking forgiveness from someone you wronged. I mentioned earlier how most people, at some point or another, will carry unforgiving feelings of resentment around things that other people did to us. For those on the spiritual path, these feelings cause tremendous conflict because we know we need to let them go, and that is often complex and difficult.

To become engaged fully in forgiving others, it is helpful to begin by taking a moment to consider times in your life when you caused pain to other people. For most of us, there will likely be several events that come to mind easily; after all, human relationships are so challenging and complex. Perhaps you didn't mean to do anything on purpose, but still, something happened that was unpleasant. Every single person alive has wronged someone either intentionally or not. When we can take a moment to dig into places where we did wrong unto others and sincerely ask another person to show us mercy and ask forgiveness, the empathy created can begin to open the door to forgiving those who have wronged us through the years.

•• ● ••
EXERCISE AND JOURNAL PROMPT
Recalling Times in the Past for Apologies

Pull out your journal and reflect on the following:

1. Think of times in the past when you may have caused situations where others need to forgive you and you need to apologize.

2. Break your life down by the decades. First, consider your childhood up to the age of ten. Next, consider your early teens, and
   then think about your twenties, and so forth.

3. Take your time to allow any and all thoughts to pour out of
   your soul without any judgment or editing.

4. Were you surprised by some of the memories that emerged
   when you concentrated on this task?

5. How beneficial will it be to receive forgiveness for those incidents you remembered?

Personal reflection is a valuable exercise to do anytime in life. You
may find more information emerges in your mind after your initial session, so consider taking more notes on this topic in the future.

Taking Stock—Time for Apology

If you're like many people, it's hard to recall what you had for break-
fast, let alone what happened months or years ago. If that journaling
exercise didn't bring much up, or even if it did, this next exercise will
allow you to travel back in time to recall places that may require someone forgiving you. You might receive more details about the items you
wrote in your journal or something new will emerge. Either way, this
is a very helpful experience. Because this is a guided journey, you may
want to record it and play it back to yourself.

•• ● ••
EXERCISE
Taking Stock—Time for Apology

Sit in your comfortable space, breathe, and relax. Bring the healing light
from head to feet, surround yourself with your golden globe of protective light, and walk through the door into your sacred space.

Your guide is already there waiting for you, and they would like to
invite you to sit and join them. Feel the unconditional love and support
your guide has for you. They're here to help you recall times when difficult things happened that others may need to forgive you for.

Speak with your guide about this now and see if they can share any other incidents or time periods they believe need to be brought to your attention. Take your time to ask any questions you need.

Pause here.

Next, allow your guide to bring out a big screen. In a moment, when you count to three, the screen will show a video of other times for you to consider. One, the screen has appeared; two, your guide is preparing your video; and three, the video begins to play. Watch the video. Notice what you notice.

Pause here.

Imagine now the video has ended and your guide is putting the screen away. Take some time to discuss what you viewed with your guide, ask questions, and receive clarity now.

Pause here.

Thank your guide for this assistance with your healing journey; say goodbye for now, stand up, and go back out the door you came through. Go out to where you began.

Surrounded by loving golden light, within this light, only that which is of your highest good can come through.

In a moment, when you count from five, you will come back into the room, feeling awake, refreshed, and better than you did before.

Five—grounded, centered, and balanced. Four—continuing to process this new energy in your dreams tonight so by tomorrow morning, you will be fully integrated into these new insights. Three—still surrounded by that beautiful golden ball of light, knowing that only that which is of your highest good can come through, you will find yourself driving carefully and being careful in all activities. Two—grounded, centered, and balanced, and one—you're back.

How did that work for you? Were you able to bring up memories you hadn't recalled before? Memory is a tapestry of complexity, so allow your mind to continue processing and recalling any other things over the next days and weeks.

•• • ••
JOURNAL PROMPT
Taking Stock—Time for Apology

Take a moment to write some notes in your journal about anything you recalled.

1. What memories did you uncover?
2. How long ago did those things happen?
3. After reviewing this, do you still feel like you owe someone an apology?
4. Were there misunderstandings that made the situation seem worse than it actually was?

Make notes about any information your parents and your guide shared that you want to recall later.

Many times, we overanalyze things that happen to the point that when we view them again, they feel different. Gaining new perspective is a major step on the path to healing. Remember to consider taking this journey again if and when you feel like doing so to address any other issues from the past you would like to resolve.

Asking for Forgiveness

Now that you've had time to review events that need healing, you will return to that same space and meet with someone you most need to meet with at this time, and you will ask for them to forgive you. In your own journaling or in that last exercise, you might have uncovered more than one situation that needs attention. If so, that's fine. You can take this journey as many times as you need. If you recorded it, then it will be easy to revisit it later. You have a choice for how to proceed.

•• • ••
EXERCISE
Asking for Forgiveness

You can either take one of the items from the list you made earlier or choose whichever event is most for your highest good. Either way, the best will emerge. Again, recording this journey may be helpful.

Sit in a comfortable chair with your feet flat on the floor and your hands in your lap. Breathe and connect with the familiar peaceful white light that moves through your entire body from head to feet. Allow that loving light to surround you now in a healing golden shield and know that within the warmth and embrace of this healing golden light, you are safe, secure, and totally protected. Very good.

Open your door and walk into your sacred space. Meet your guide and say hello. Let your guide know that you would like to ask someone for forgiveness today. Explain the situation to your guide. Let them know who you would like to meet today, or let your guide know that you request whoever or whatever is for your highest good.

Pause here.

Notice now the doorway on the other side of your sacred space. That door is opening and here comes the person or people you will meet with today. Know that this is their Higher Self or soul essence. Say hello and notice they are happy to see you. Take your time to discuss the situation with them and apologize. Have whatever conversation you need.

Pause here.

Imagine the person or people are more than willing to accept your apology. Allow them to express this to you in a way that brings greater peace and joy to your heart and mind.

Pause here.

Thank them for joining you today and say goodbye. Wish them well as they walk or float back through the door. Turn to your personal guide and speak with them about any insights or further information you need to put this situation to rest and enjoy a successful conclusion to this issue.

Pause here.

Thank your guide for assisting you today. Say goodbye and watch while they float away. Turn around and go back out the door you entered. Close the door and be back now. Still surrounded by that golden, protective ball of light, in a moment, when you count back from five, you will return, feeling awake, refreshed, and better than ever before.

Five—processing this healing in your dreams tonight. Four—knowing that greater inner peace awaits in your future. Three—you're grounded, centered, and balanced. Two—knowing by tomorrow morning, you will be fully integrated into this new energy, and one—you're back.

This is another journey that could be quite emotional, so be sure and take good care of yourself. After emerging from your inner world, you may benefit from going outside, taking a walk in nature, calling a friend, or retreating into a warm bath as you take time to process. Remember that although this exchange occurred in your imagination, powerful changes can emerge in three-dimensional reality because of your efforts.

•• • ••

JOURNAL PROMPT
Asking for Forgiveness

Take your time to record anything important. Here are a few questions to get you going.

1. Did you meet with the person you intended to or did someone else show up?
2. What did you say to them when you apologized?
3. How did they react?
4. Were you surprised by their reaction?
5. Did they forgive you?
6. How can this experience help you in the future?

Remember that forgiveness is a journey, not a destination, so if you feel you have more to heal, that's okay. Even the slightest shift in your feelings about the past can be a hugely beneficial step to getting yourself going in a positive new direction. Taking the time to ask another person to extend grace to you for things that happened in the past can be a humbling and healing experience. By allowing yourself to become vulnerable in this way, you may be open to making more room to forgive other people who would also like to receive the gift of forgiveness from you. Also, if nothing happened or if you didn't receive the desired outcome, that's okay. Again, take time to nurture yourself and allow the healing to unfold slowly.

Forgiving Others

You already did a short journey to receive forgiveness and unconditional love from your parents. You also asked others to forgive you. In reality, there are potentially dozens of times in our lives when others wronged us, so now you're going to experience a broader journey to assist you in forgiving others. Earlier, I provided a list of several of the possible people you may need to forgive. This includes family, friends, coworkers, strangers...the list is endless.

Despite the potentially horrible behavior and actions that human beings often perpetuate against each other, I still like to believe that most people are doing the best they can at any given time. That said, some things are absolutely inexcusable, and cases of pure evil do exist. More often though, misunderstandings happen when well-meaning people don't get things right. You may have uncovered that during the exercises in the previous chapter. When you thought about your motivations for what happened, I would imagine that more often than not, you never intended ill will or harm. That is a good frame of reference to consider as you dive into this next section.

•• ● ••

EXERCISE AND JOURNAL PROMPT
Recalling Times to Forgive Others

As you did in the previous exercise, I invite you to get your journal out.

1. Write out anything you can recall about situations you need to forgive.

2. Review the first decade of your life, your teens, twenties, and so forth.

3. Take your time and let all the details, feelings, and emotions come out on the page.

4. Who was involved and what happened?

5. Do you believe you could forgive these incidents? If not, that's okay. The simple act of writing them down is a great start.

Write anything else that may be helpful. Once that's done, if you believe there still might be more to uncover, you can take the guided journey to uncover more events or new information and details about the things you most need to forgive.

Taking Stock—Forgiving Others

Top-of-mind incidents that you can easily recall don't need guided imagery, but to receive more details about those things or to recall other times that may need your energy and attention, it's helpful to use your inner world to bring up those items. Next, you can enlist your special guide to assist you in recalling more hidden memories of things you may need to forgive. This will be a simple and fast exercise. You could glance over this one and then take the journey or record it in advance—your choice.

•• ● ••
EXERCISE
Taking Stock—Forgiving Others

Sit in a comfortable seat, close your eyes, and breathe. Allow healing white light to pour forth from head to feet, moving into every single cell in your body. Allow that light to stream out of your heart center and surround you in a protective golden shell. Within your golden light, you are safe, secure, and protected.

Notice the door into your sacred space. Open that door now and go inside your sanctuary. Your guide is waiting for you and invites you to take a seat; notice the video screen they've prepared for you. Speak to your loving guide about helping you recall any deeper memories of situations you would like to release in the energy of forgiveness. Take your time to have that conversation; receive their unconditional love and support.

Pause here.

Very nice. Your guide is now going to play a video. Allow the video to show you any times that most need healing at this moment in your life's journey. Take your time to notice all you can.

Pause here.

When you're ready, the video stops. Speak to your guide about what you saw and allow them to share helpful insights.

Pause here.

Thank your guide for their assistance today. Stand up and walk or float back to the door you came through. Say goodbye and go out to where you began, closing that door behind you. You're grounded, centered, and balanced, and in a moment, when you count from five, you will come back into the room, feeling awake, refreshed, and better than you did before.

Five—grounded, centered, and balanced. Four—you will process this information in your dreams tonight so by tomorrow morning, you will be fully integrated into these new insights. Three—surrounded by that beautiful golden ball of light, knowing that only that which is of your highest good can come through, you will find yourself driving carefully and being careful in all activities. Two—grounded, centered, and balanced, and one—you're back.

Recalling forgotten challenges can ultimately bring them to the forefront of the mind and begin the process of resolving these incidents.

•• ● ••
JOURNAL PROMPT
Taking Stock—Forgiving Others

Make a few important notes about your journey that can help you later.

1. What memories, if any, did your guide help you recall?

2. Which of those seemed most important to you?

3. Do you think you could forgive these situations?

Bringing up these challenging situations can be tough for people. Once you do this though, it can yield incredibly powerful results in terms of your own healing. Again, if you cannot forgive something, that is perfectly okay.

Forgiving People from Your Past

Now that you've worked to recall certain events, this next journey is designed so you can meet face-to-face with the people involved in your most pressing difficulties and have conversations with them that perhaps you haven't had a chance to in real life. Because most of us have so many issues to resolve, know that you can take this journey again and again while holding different people and situations in mind and receive new results.

Before you begin, you may want to go through the notes you made in the last two exercises and decide which issue feels the most pressing at this moment. Also remember that when you forgive, that is often a slow process. You may not be able to totally release something, but the goal is to make incremental progress to help you slowly feel better about these challenges and ultimately make more room for your own spirit to soar and inner peace to abound.

Remember also that whoever you meet with will be coming to you at a soul level and you will interact with their Higher Self. At this level, they can provide you with the needed apologies and support that can help you heal and move on. Record this journey for best results.

•• ● ••
EXERCISE
Forgiving People from Your Past

Find your outer sanctuary where you do your spiritual work, sit, close your eyes, and relax. Take a deep and healing breath in through your nose as you invite a healing white light to pour down from above. That light heals your body, mind, and spirit as it moves into every single cell of your being. Moving into your head and neck, your arms and body, and into your legs and feet, the light carries away tensions and concerns. Feel the loving light surrounding and protecting you with a golden shield and remember only that which is of your highest good can come through.

Open your door and step inside your sacred space. Your guide is there. Take your time to tell them who you wish to meet today. You may also choose to allow whoever is for your highest good to show up. Your guide will remind you that whoever arrives will be meeting you as their soul essence or Higher Self.

Pause here.

When you're ready, you notice a doorway on the other side of your sacred space. That door is opening now, and here comes the person you wish to see today or someone who is most for your highest good to meet with.

Notice that person or people now. They are walking or floating out to see you and imagine they are happy to see you today and so pleased to join you. Take a moment while they speak to you and apologize about the events that went on in the past. Know that at this Higher Self level, they are truly sorry for causing you pain. They want you to know they were doing the best they could at the time, and they seek your forgiveness today. Take your time to have this conversation and tell them how you felt about this. Get it all out and discuss everything.

Pause here.

Take a moment now and let them know if you can forgive them today or not. If so, do that now; if not, could you feel at least a little bit better about this situation? If so, great, but if not, what would you need from them to feel a little better? Know that they are willing to give you what you need. Take your time to discuss all of this now.

Pause here.

Very good. Now imagine they can once again express their remorse about what happened. They send you unconditional love and peace today as they say goodbye and walk or float back through the door they came through. Take a moment to speak with your guide about the healing they sent you today.

Pause here.

Thank your loving guide again, say goodbye, and walk or float back through the door you came through.

In a moment, when you count from five, you will come back into the room, feeling awake, refreshed, and better than you did before.

Five—grounded, centered, and balanced. Four—continuing to process this new energy in your dreams tonight so by tomorrow morning, you will be fully integrated into these new insights. Three—still surrounded by that beautiful golden ball of light, knowing that only that which is of your highest good can come through, you will find yourself driving carefully and being careful in all activities. Two—grounded, centered, and balanced, and one—you're back.

This forgiveness business is not the easiest thing to do, but your future happiness can be greatly expanded through your effort. Again, remember that even if you could not forgive someone, bringing your feelings about the situation into your conscious awareness helps.

•• • ••

JOURNAL PROMPT
Forgiving People from Your Past

Take time to record your feelings and progress in your journal. You will be fascinated to review this later as you notice what shifts and changes.

1. Who did you intend to meet with today?
2. Did that person show up or did you see someone else?
3. What happened in the past that you needed to forgive?
4. How did they react to what you said? Did they apologize?
5. How did their apology or reaction make you feel?
6. Did you feel you made progress in letting go of old energy by forgiving?

Please take your time to make any other notes and record what you observed. Be sure to write out all the details as you remember them to aid in the healing process and describe how you explained your situation to the person you met with and how they responded.

Again, while you may not have achieved a full resolution the first time out, the goal is to make progress, even if it's slight. Every step you take toward releasing stuck energy will bring you greater light and love in your current situation as you move forward on the path of healing. Even the slightest shift in awareness is an amazing accomplishment. And even if you could not forgive, the courage you showed in looking into this issue is amazing. When we heal ourselves, we assist all of humanity, past, present, and future. The energy you put into establishing inner peace about the past through the journey of forgiveness can pay huge dividends in the future. I applaud your efforts in forgiveness and encourage you to continue.

Forgiving Yourself

So far, you asked others to extend grace and forgiveness for any wrongs you did in the past, then you attempted to hear others out and extend that same light to them. Now it's time for the truly tough stuff—the challenge of forgiving the one person who everyone needs to learn to love more than anyone else—*yourself.*

To better facilitate your ability for Ancestral Healing as well as greater happiness in all areas of life, it's time to let go of the past and extend compassion and grace to yourself. Doing so will help you move into an energy of knowing that all your so-called mistakes can be wonderful opportunities for soul growth. That concept is often easier said than done, right? This isn't easy work.

Why is the task of loving and forgiving ourselves so hard? That, my friend, is a question for the ages. Most of us live with regret about things done or not done, opportunities missed, mistakes made. It's incredibly easy to beat ourselves up over a wide variety of issues. That said, what if the things that happen to us in our lives really do happen for a reason? Do you think that's possible? I do. At least I've come to that conclusion after many years.

This is not easy stuff to digest though. What if that thing you thought you had to have simply wasn't for you? What if something better really did show up? What if the timing wasn't right and down the road things worked out anyway? There are unlimited possibilities, and I have come to embrace the idea that things are going as planned. The plan may not be how you would have created it now that you have hindsight on your side, but there is a divine plan and things do work out in divine order. Forgiving yourself for perceived mistakes opens your energy to receive the bounty of the Divine in all areas of your life. Everybody makes mistakes. That's how we learn, yet sometimes the mistakes from our past haunt our present and make life miserable. Before you can heal those events, you must first recall them.

• • ● • •

EXERCISE AND JOURNAL PROMPT
Forgiving Yourself

Now it's time to pull out your journal again.

1. Make some notes about things in your past that upset you, only this time, the person who upset you is the same one you must face in the mirror every day—yourself.

2. Consider time periods in your life again. Pause and reflect on stages of your life and upsetting things that happened during your childhood until age ten, your teens, twenties, and so forth.

3. Recall times when you reached out and missed, lost or failed, or were misunderstood. Take all the time you need to compassionately recall what you can and make notes.

4. Can you see in hindsight that you did your best?

5. Do you think you can find the energy to release your anger at yourself and recognize the learning and soul gifts provided by these experiences?

Throughout this chapter, I've encouraged you to know that it's okay if you cannot forgive, and that applies to this exercise as well. Even if you can make the tiniest progress in letting go of upset feelings you have about your past, that's a good thing. You deserve happiness and love and with steady progress, you can move forward on the path to self-love and forgiveness.

Taking Stock—Forgiving Yourself

Once again, you will go on a guided journey to see if any more details emerge that can help your healing journey. You will once again enlist the help of your loving guide to assist you in uncovering some of the wounds that most need healing. I recommend recording this journey.

•• ● ••
EXERCISE
Taking Stock—Forgiving Yourself

Retreat to your comfortable space. Close your eyes. Relax and breathe, inhaling peace and love and joy, and exhaling any tensions and concerns. Allow yourself to feel a loving pure white light that moves through your body from head to feet. Allow the light to heal every cell in your body as it moves through your head, arms, body, and legs. Feel the light pouring out your heart and surrounding you in healing golden light. Know you are safe, protected, and embraced within this golden light now and always.

Notice the door that leads to your sacred space. Open the door now and walk or float into your beautiful room. Your guide is there waiting for you. Let them know you would like help uncovering things that you're most angry at yourself about. Your guide welcomes you to sit in a comfortable seat and they bring out a video screen. Sit down now and take a moment to discuss this with your guide.

Pause here.

Now your guide will play a video to help you uncover the places most in need of healing. Watch the video, notice all you can, and when you're done, ask your guide for any clarity.

Pause here.

Thank your guide for their loving assistance today. They turn off the video and you are now free to get up and go back out to where you began your journey. Close the door behind you and be back now where you started. Still surrounded by golden light, safe and secure, in a moment, when you count from five, you will come back into the room, feeling awake, refreshed, and better than you did before.

Five—grounded, centered, and balanced. Four—continuing to process this new energy in your dreams tonight so by tomorrow morning, you will be fully integrated into these new insights. Three—still surrounded by that beautiful golden ball of light, knowing that only that which is of your highest good can come through, you will find yourself driving carefully and being careful in all activities. Two—grounded, centered, and balanced, and one—you're back.

Did you recall anything new, or did you gain further clarity on things you already remembered?

•• • ••

JOURNAL PROMPT
Taking Stock—Forgiving Yourself

Make a few notes about the information you received. Here are a few ideas.

1. What information emerged?
2. How can you use the information received to bring healing to your life?

3. What guidance did your guide offer you that will help you on this journey toward self-acceptance and healing?

These challenges can run within the depths of our souls. Go gentle on yourself and pat yourself on the back for taking time to take stock and move forward on your healing journey.

Forgiving Your Younger Self

Now that you've worked on bringing specific situations to mind, when you're ready, you can take the following journey to heal those issues. To do this process, you will meet with the younger you who likely did the best they could at the time. The two of you can discuss what happened and hopefully come to a new understanding about your past. You may have certain situations that are too tender to touch right now, so do what feels best to you. You could also allow whichever situation comes up during the journey to be the one you look at. It's all up to you. Record this exercise for greater ease.

•• • ••
EXERCISE
Forgiving Your Younger Self

Sit in your sacred space, prepare in any way you wish to feel supported, and when you're ready, close your eyes. Breathe. Relax and imagine a beautiful healing light coming down through the top of your head. Feel that light moving through your body, your arms and legs, and allow the light to carry any tensions from your body into the earth. The light becomes stronger and surrounds you in golden protective light.

Notice the door that leads into your sacred space. Open the door now and walk or float into your beautiful room. Take a moment to receive the beneficial and supportive energies of your special place. As you absorb those positive vibrations, notice your guide is floating down to join you. Say hello and let your guide know that you would like to engage in the amazing process of self-forgiveness. Let your guide know which specific issue you have in mind or allow them to share information that might help you decide what to work on, or you might let them assist you with allowing your highest good to emerge during this process.

Pause here.

When you're ready, notice the doorway on the other side of your room is opening. Here comes the younger you, the version of yourself who engaged in the activity you've had a hard time letting go of over the years. Say hello to your younger self and allow them to explain the situation to you. Allow the younger you to tell you their rationale for why they did what they did and why they made decisions or took actions in that moment.

Pause here.

Imagine you can now understand more fully the reasons why this happened, or if you had no control over what occurred, imagine now it's so much easier to recognize this in the present. Take a moment to express to your younger you any wisdom you gained or new perspectives you now have as you're older and share that insight and grace with your younger self now. Take your time to say all you wish and allow your younger self to respond accordingly.

Pause here.

Very nice. Imagine now you can forgive yourself for what happened. Tell the younger you that although this wasn't the best situation, you're now ready to accept what happened and forgive yourself. If you feel guided, you could also hug your younger self and offer them words of support and encouragement. Let them know what they have waiting for them and assure them all is well.

Pause here.

When you're ready, thank the younger you for joining you today for this healing. Notice now they are saying goodbye and thanking you for this meeting and walking or floating back through the door they came through. Turn to your guide. Allow your guide a moment to share their insights about this situation and talk to them about anything else you'd like to discuss.

Pause here.

Thank your guide for helping you again. They're saying goodbye for now and floating away. Take a moment to fill yourself with the loving energy of your special room. Turn now with this new energy and walk or float back through the door, closing that door behind you, and go out to where you began.

Still surrounded by that golden ball of light and now filled with new insights and wisdom beyond anything you've ever felt before, notice how peaceful you feel in this new energy. In a moment, when you count from five, you will come back into the room, feeling awake, refreshed, and better than you did before.

Five—grounded, centered, and balanced. Four—continuing to process this new energy in your dreams tonight so by tomorrow morning, you will be fully integrated into these new insights. Three—still surrounded by that beautiful golden ball of light, knowing that only that which is of your highest good can come through, you will find yourself driving carefully and being careful in all activities. Two—grounded, centered, and balanced, and one—you're back.

You did it! Congratulations on taking this important step to self-healing. That might have felt difficult, so if needed, take a break, and go do something you enjoy.

· · ● · ·
JOURNAL PROMPT
Forgiving Your Younger Self

Now that you've faced the past, consider the following:

1. What event did you uncover today that you needed to forgive yourself for?

2. How did it feel to extend grace to your younger self?

3. What insights did you gain by uncovering your younger self's motivation for doing what they did?

4. Did you forgive yourself?

5. How did forgiveness make you feel?

Now that you've completed this exercise, I encourage you to keep track of your feelings and make note of any improvements you notice after a week. While the forgiveness of others is transformative, letting go of self-resentment can also make some hugely beneficial shifts in your energy field. Noticing those benefits will help you continue your journey and the path toward healing. If possible, find compassion for the younger you and know you did your best with what you dealt with at the time.

Summing Up

Forgiveness is perhaps the toughest and greatest lesson we humans need to learn. In our current third-dimensional consciousness, we've been trained to view things in a world of duality. Every person alive experiences tough times, and many of those are caused by other people, whether intentionally or not. A huge factor in achieving peace in life comes from releasing the stagnant energy around past events. Participating in forgiveness exercises will free your energy to receive more love, joy, peace, and happiness now and in the future.

As we learn and grow, overcoming obstacles to raise our vibrational frequencies above the "us versus them" mentality means we let go and release the challenges of the past to embrace a brighter future. Once you set your heart at peace by practicing forgiveness, you'll be far better prepared to move into the next phase of Ancestral Energy Healing by working on your energy fields and taking more powerful guided journeys.

Remember to extend grace and forgiveness to yourself if you fail at these beginning attempts to forgive yourself and others. The mere act of trying to open to that possibility makes positive lasting change for the better. Healing and forgiveness may not happen, or they may unfold slowly over time. That's okay and perfect. Go easy on yourself and know all is well.

CHAPTER FOUR
. . . .
Ancestral Genealogical Regressions

I will now move to the heart of the work of Ancestral Energy Healing with the Genealogical Regression process I developed years ago to help people who needed to heal current-life familial problems before under-going their past-life regression. There were times when I knew—before people could even begin to go into events that happened to their souls hundreds or maybe even thousands of years ago—that first they needed to go do some forgiveness work or other healing with their immediate family. Many times that involved spouses or siblings, but it also involved meeting with their parents.

Over time, this evolved into asking parents if either of them felt their family needed a healing. The answer to that question was always yes, so instead of having clients imagining themselves floating into their own past events, they experienced events that happened to their ancestors.

By accessing these early ancestral events, healing can be sent, and the ripple effects of the high-frequency light the ancestors receive make a positive impact on the person sending the healing as well as on all members of their family. Because the entire family line is lightened through this technique, that healing vibration continues to ripple out into the future and therefore makes a positive impact on those who have yet to be born. There are a few important considerations about Genealogical Regression I would like to briefly review.

- **Work at your own pace**—Regardless of how you did on the parental forgiveness section, you can, if you choose, move forward with the Genealogical Regression. The conversation could be as simple as asking briefly if the family needs healing. You can always work on deeper layers of forgiveness sometime in the future. The parental figure simply opens the door to allow you to explore those ancestors who lived in early times.

- **Defining the term** *parent*—You are in charge of your journey, and you decide which parental figure or caregiver appears to work with you on these healings. That could include birth parents, adoptive parents, foster caregivers, grandparents, and so forth.

- **Higher Selves of parents**—The other key to remember here is that you will be engaging with the Higher Self or soul essence of each parent you encounter. Addressing people at the soul level enables truly transformative outcomes to emerge over time.

Because the soul is so complex, you might also find it helpful to do these more than once. With the deep soul connections and ties you have with your parents, there could be more than one thing to exchange. Likewise, do the journey for any and all parental or influential people you have in your life.

Soul Retrieval with Parental Figures

Speaking of your parents, now that you've engaged in forgiveness with them, the next deepening of this process is to engage in something called Soul Retrieval. In past-life regression experiences, your soul may need to heal with other souls by taking back items that belong to you or releasing things you no longer need or that were thrust upon you in the past. What are these things you give and receive? They are as varied and unique as each one of us. Sometimes the exchange can involve objects such as a jewelry box or a symbol or amulet. Other times the exchange involves what I have always called a virtue such as love or forgiveness or grace or courage—all things you cannot see but you can surely feel. There is no limit to what you may encounter as you ask for what's yours and give back things that no longer serve you. The results are as unique and varied as the stars in the sky.

During these exchanges, you may see the items as the other person presents them, but more importantly, you *feel* them. When you take things back inside yourself, a healing occurs—a real energy shift that can be quite profound. Normally even when there's an object, it represents a virtue or something of a higher nature that helps you in your life and energizes you on a spiritual level.

When you give back the things that are not serving you or that you're carrying around for others, that can be equally, if not more, powerful. There is a distinct sense of a heavy weight being lifted off your soul as you put down your burdens and give them back to the person they truly belong to. When we took out the trash earlier, you likely felt a sense of lightness and ease. This process is similar. It's so common for all of us to take on things for others. In society, that is theoretically a good thing to do to be of service, yet when those items are not for us to carry, doing too much can be detrimental to our own well-being and soul growth.

Giving and receiving in this loving way is beneficial on a karmic level for both you and the person you're doing the exchange with because the person is normally so happy to receive their things back, you notice an energetic shift within them that is quite profound at times. As with all the journeys, remember, I am giving you a summation of over twenty years of experience with this process. You are a one-in-a-billion individual with your own soul journey to go through, and so what is given or received may be even more amazing than what I can describe. Another possibility is that you won't need to give or receive anything at all. If that happens, which it does often, you will exchange love, the best gift any of us can ever share with each other.

Using Soul Retrieval for Ancestral Energy Healing is incredibly powerful because, unlike our karma and past lives, the ancestors and lineages have undoubtedly given you things to carry through the ages. As many people who embrace Ancestral Healing are now finding, those burdens become increasingly heavy as we go through life. Take back things that belong to you from your parents, give things back to them that you do not need. Your parents will also be giving and receiving things from you. In this version, you will also release things that specifically relate to your lineage and ancestors.

Soul Retrieval with a Maternal Figure

Because this work can be emotional, the exercises will be divided so you can do the Soul Retrieval with your mother or other maternal figure and father or other paternal figure separately. First, you will go meet with the maternal figure of your choice and see what she wants to exchange with you. As with all the journeys here, this can be emotional, particularly if the person you meet with is deceased or if there's an issue between you. If you don't feel guided to do this journey, that's fine. I highly recommend recording these to help you go deeper into the process. In this journey, I will refer to the maternal figure as your mom or mother for the sake of simplicity, but know this term applies to anyone maternal in your life.

•• • ••
EXERCISE
Soul Retrieval with a Maternal Figure

Sit in a comfortable chair with your hands in your lap and feet flat on the floor. Close your eyes. Breathe. Take a deep, healing breath in through your nose, breathing in love and peace and light. Exhale any tensions and concerns. Continue to breathe, and as you do, you find yourself becoming more and more relaxed. Feel the breath going into your body. Imagine you are breathing in love, and joy, and relaxation, and peace, and you continue to exhale tensions and concerns. Very good. Continue to breathe and count as you do so, noticing that as you count and breathe, your state of inner peace is relaxing more and more. Ready?

Breathing in peace, joy, and love and exhaling tensions. Continue to breathe. With each breath you take, you are becoming more and more relaxed. Find yourself breathing in peace, joy, and love as you release tensions and concerns.

Imagine a beautiful beam of pure white light coming down through the top of your head. Feel that light moving through your head and forehead, floating into your eyes, your nose, your mouth, and your jaw.

Continue to breathe as the light moves down, down, down, down, through your neck and shoulders, into your arms, your elbows, your wrists, your hands and fingertips.

Feel the light as it continues flowing down, down, down into your shoulders, your collarbone, your shoulder blades, and continues to flow down, down, down, into your heart center. Feel your heart energy expand as the light continues to move down into your stomach, traveling down, down, down your spine and into your lungs, flowing down to the base of your spine. Continue to breathe as this loving light moves down, down, down, through the base of your spine, flowing into your legs—your thighs, your knees, your calves, your ankles and heels, and down into the soles of your feet and into your toes.

Imagine the light is getting stronger now as it moves from the crown of your head, all the way down through your body, through your spine, through your legs and down and out the soles of your feet. The light is becoming stronger now, so strong it begins to pour out of your heart center, creating a beautiful golden ball of light that surrounds you by about three feet in all directions. Imagine feeling yourself floating inside this peaceful golden ball of light. Know that within this golden ball of light, you are safe, secure, and totally carefree, and know that within the golden light, only that which is of your highest good can come through.

Notice your doorway in front of you. When you count back from three, you will walk through that door and go inside a beautiful room, a sacred space where you can feel totally relaxed, nurtured, and protected.

Ready? Three, two, one; you're opening the door. Open the door now. Walk or float inside your sacred space. Be there now and notice that your loving guide is floating down to meet you. Say hello and let them know you are here to meet with your mother's Higher Self to do Soul Retrieval. Take a moment to speak with your guide now.

Pause here.

Turn your attention to the doorway you've seen before. That door is opening, and your mom's Higher Self is walking or floating through the door. Notice how happy she is to see you. She's so grateful to you for the work you are doing with Ancestral Healing. Take a moment to discuss anything you would like to speak with her about.

Pause here.

When you're ready, imagine your mother standing right in front of you, peaceful and relaxed, and she's sending you so much love. Imagine you can ask your mother if she has anything she would like to give to you that would be of benefit to you in the future. The gift may or may not be something that belonged to your ancestors, but regardless, it will be of great value to you. If she does have something to share, imagine she is putting it out on the palms of her hands now. Know that whatever she may have for you can be an object, or it may be a virtue such as courage or strength. Take your time to notice this and if needed, imagine either she or your loving guide can help you know exactly what this is you're receiving. If she doesn't have anything specific, allow her to send her love to you now.

Pause here.

Notice the gift. What is it? Does this relate to your ancestors, and if so, how? If the gift is an object, imagine your mother can tell you what that object represents. Notice that now and imagine it is easy for you to understand what the object represents. If it is a virtue such as courage, allow her to explain why you received this, and if she does not have anything for you specifically, allow her to send you love.

Pause here.

As you receive the gift, imagine you can pick it up now and put it right inside your heart. Feel your mother's gift as it moves into your heart center and begins to flow down, down, down through your body into your legs and feet, and moves up, up, up, through your shoulders, arms, neck, and head. Feel the loving intentions of this gift as it energizes and refreshes you. You are becoming lighter and lighter and lighter, brighter and brighter and brighter, so light and bright, feeling better than ever before. Your mother is also receiving this healing and she is becoming lighter and lighter.

Pause here.

When you're ready, imagine you can look inside yourself and notice if you have anything that belongs to your mom. This could be something that belongs to her, a duty, or a burden you've been carrying for her. Know that she welcomes and encourages you to return this to her and to free yourself from these burdens. You may also give her love or any other virtue you see fit. Take a moment and put this out on your hands.

Pause here.

Imagine you can explain to your mother what this gift represents or if it's something you've been carrying for her; you can have a meaningful conversation about this energy, and she can thank you for taking it on and for now giving it back. If this is an object, what does it represent? If it is a virtue such as forgiveness, take your time to give this to her and speak with her about whatever you need to say. If you don't feel you have anything for her, you can give her love.

Pause here.

When you're ready, you can hand the gift to your mother. Notice she is picking it up, lifting it from you and putting it right inside her heart. As she does this, notice you are feeling lighter and lighter and lighter, brighter and brighter, so much better than before. You are no longer burdened by what you're giving back.

As your mother receives this gift, she is getting lighter and lighter as well as the energy of your gift moves through her heart center, through her body, and into her mind. She is receiving this healing and she is so grateful to you for this special gift.

As the two of you receive this healing and light, imagine your loving guide is there with you both and brings out that golden pair of scissors. As they do, you can notice an energetic cord is connecting you and your mother. This cord represents all that has gone on in the past—the good and the bad. In a moment, when you count to three, your guide will cut that cord and send you both a high-frequency healing light that will strengthen your relationship even more. This light will be received in the spirit of knowing that the past is the past, all is forgiven, and the two of you can move forward together in greater harmony. If your mother is in spirit, know this healing can be just as powerful and meaningful as if she were still alive. Now your guide will cut that cord and send you both this healing. Ready? One, two, and three; your guide is cutting that cord now.

A gorgeous beam of pure white healing light is pouring down through you both, through the tops of your heads, your necks, arms, wrists, hands, and fingers, and it's flowing through your bodies into your legs and feet. You are both becoming lighter and lighter and brighter than ever before, the bonds of love and peace stronger now than they ever have been between you. Take your time as you both receive this healing light.

Pause here.

When you're ready, imagine your mom thanks you so much for this energy exchange. She may hug you or speak with you to express her gratitude. Take a moment to receive and exchange this and allow her and your guide to tell you anything else you need to know about the gifts you received today.

Pause here.

Very good. Now notice how much lighter and brighter your mother appears than when you began this journey today. She is letting you know she loves you. Feel the unconditional love your mom has for you. Even if you've never felt this before in your waking life, feel that love now.

Pause here.

Very nice. Say goodbye for now and imagine she can walk or float back through the door she came through. You're there with your guide, and if needed, you can ask your guide for any further clarity or insights.

Pause here.

When you're finished, imagine you can thank your guide for being here today and watch your guide float up, up, up, floating back to where they came from. Know you will see your guide again soon.

Take a deep breath in through your nose. Breathe in one, two, three, four, and exhale one, two, three, and four as you allow yourself to become completely relaxed inside your sacred space. Filled with peaceful light and the gifts you received from your mother, having released energies you no longer need, you're feeling better than you did before. Turn around now and walk back through the door to where you began your journey. Be there now, back where you began. Close that door behind you and know you will return to your sacred space very soon.

In a moment, when you count from five, you will come back into the room, feeling awake, refreshed, and better than you did before.

Five—grounded, centered, and balanced. Four—continuing to process this new energy in your dreams tonight so by tomorrow morning, you will be fully integrated into these new insights. Three—still surrounded by that beautiful golden ball of light, knowing that only that which is of your highest good can come through, you will find yourself driving carefully and being careful in all activities. Two—grounded, centered, and balanced, and one—you're back.

How do you feel?

• • ● • •
JOURNAL PROMPT
Soul Retrieval with a Maternal Figure

That was quite a journey to perform such an amazing spiritual exchange with the motherly figure in your life. I encourage you to make a few notes. Here are some suggestions.

1. What did your mother or maternal caregiver share with you today?
2. What did you give to her?
3. Did your gifts involve your ancestors? If so, how?
4. How can you use the gifts you received to improve your future?
5. How did this exchange free up your energy to create greater peace in your life?

Receiving unconditional love from a parental figure can be incredibly emotional. Take good care of yourself as you process this journey. Get something to eat, go outside and enjoy the day, or do other nurturing things to care for yourself.

Soul Retrieval with a Paternal Figure

When you're ready, you can take a similar journey to the one you just completed with your mother or maternal figure and find out what items, if any, you need to exchange with your dad, your father, or another paternal figure in your life. Like before, I will refer to this individual as your dad or father, but know that this applies to anyone who played that role in your life.

• • ● • •
EXERCISE
Soul Retrieval with a Paternal Figure

Sit again in your comfortable place, close your eyes, relax, and connect with healing light that moves through your entire body. When you're ready, walk through the door and return to your inner sacred space.

Your loving guide greets you there. Let them know you are seeking an energy exchange and Soul Retrieval with your father. Take a moment to share anything you would like to with your guide now.

Pause here.

Very good. Now you notice your father or another paternal or father figure is approaching you so the two of you can exchange gifts and receive a mutual healing.

When you're ready, imagine your father steps right in front of you, peaceful and relaxed. Imagine you can ask your father if he has anything he would like to give to you that would be of benefit to you in the future. The gift may or may not be something that belonged to your ancestors, but regardless, it will be of great value to you. If he does, imagine he puts it in your hands now. This may be an object or a virtue such as courage. Take your time to notice and know that either your father or your loving guide will help you understand what you're receiving. If he doesn't have anything specific, allow him to send you love.

Pause here.

Notice the gift. What is it? Does this relate to your ancestors, and if so, how? If the gift is an object, imagine your father tells you what that object represents. Notice that now and imagine it is easy for you to understand. If it is a virtue such as courage, allow him to explain why he gave that to you, and if there isn't anything specific he has for you, receive his love.

Pause here.

As you receive the gift from your father, imagine you can pick it up and put the gift right inside your heart. Feel your dad's gift as it moves into your heart center and begins to flow down, down, down through your body into your legs and feet, and moves up, up, up, through your shoulders, arms, neck, and head. Feel the loving intentions of his gift as it energizes and refreshes you. You are becoming lighter and lighter and lighter, brighter and brighter and brighter, so light and bright, feeling better than ever before. Your father is also receiving this healing and he is becoming lighter and lighter.

Pause here.

When you're ready, imagine you can look inside yourself and notice if you have anything that belongs to your dad. This could be something that belongs to him specifically, a duty, or a burden you've been carrying for him. Notice he encourages you to return this to him and to free yourself from these burdens. You may also send love or any other virtue you see fit. Take a moment and put this gift of the spirit out on your hands.

Pause here.

Imagine you can explain what this gift represents or if it's something you've been carrying around for him; have a meaningful conversation about this energy. Imagine he thanks you for taking it on and for now giving it back. If this is an object, what does the object represent? If this is a virtue such as forgiveness, take your time and speak with him and express whatever you need to say. If you don't feel you have anything for him, you can send love.

Pause here.

When you're ready, you can hand the gift to your father. Notice he picks it up, lifting it from you and putting it right inside his heart. As he does this, you are becoming lighter and lighter and lighter, brighter and brighter, feeling so much better than before. You are no longer burdened by what you're giving back.

As your dad receives this gift, he gets lighter and lighter as the energy of your gift moves through his heart center, through his entire body and mind. He receives this healing and is so grateful to you for this special gift.

As the two of you receive this healing and light, imagine your loving guide brings out that golden pair of scissors. As they do, you notice an energetic cord is connecting you and your father. This cord represents all that has gone on in the past—the good and the bad. In a moment, when you count to three, your guide will cut that cord and send you both a high-frequency healing light that will strengthen your relationship even more. This light will be received in the spirit of knowing that the past is the past, all is forgiven, and the two of you can move forward together in greater harmony. If your dad or father figure is in spirit, know that this healing can be just as powerful and meaningful as if he were still alive. Your guide will cut that cord and send you both this healing. Ready? One, two, and three; your guide is cutting that cord now.

A gorgeous beam of pure white healing light is pouring down through you both, flowing through your heads, your necks, arms, wrists, hands, and fingers, moving through your bodies and into your legs and feet. You are both becoming lighter and lighter and brighter than ever before; the bonds of love and peace are stronger now than they ever have been between you. Take your time as you both receive this healing light.

Pause here.

When you're ready, imagine your dad thanks you for this energy exchange and he expresses his gratitude. Take a moment while he and your guide tell you anything else you need to know about the gifts you received today.

Pause here.

Very good. Now notice how much lighter and brighter your father appears now than he did when you began this journey. Feel the unconditional love and high regard your dad has for you. Even if you've never felt this before in your waking life, feel that love now.

Pause here.

Very nice. Say goodbye for now and imagine he walks back through the door he came through. Take a moment to ask your guide for any further clarity or insights.

Pause here.

Thank your guide for being here today. Turn around and walk back through the door to where you began your journey. Be there now, back where you began. Close that door behind you and know you will be back there again very soon.

In a moment, when you count from five, you will come back into the room, feeling awake, refreshed, and better than you did before.

Five—grounded, centered, and balanced. Four—continuing to process this new energy in your dreams tonight so by tomorrow morning, you will be fully integrated into these new insights. Three—still surrounded by that beautiful golden ball of light, knowing that only that which is of your highest good can come through, you will find yourself driving carefully and being careful in all activities. Two—grounded, centered, and balanced, and one—you're back.

• • ● • •
JOURNAL PROMPT
Soul Retrieval with a Paternal Figure

Congratulations on engaging in a Soul Retrieval with your father. Take notes about the items you received and gave away. Here are a few ideas of where to begin.

1. What did your father give you?
2. What did you give to him?
3. Did your gifts involve your ancestors? If so, how?
4. How can you use the gifts you received to improve your future?

As usual, make any other notes you would like. Also, if emotions emerged, take time to acknowledge your feelings, both good and bad, and know that's okay.

I would imagine both journeys you took with your mother and father figures proved quite emotional. If so, take time to process and care for yourself by doing fun activities you enjoy. While the journeys may have been emotional, I also hope they yielded some amazing insights. Congratulations for doing this work. This will be of tremendous benefit to you as you move through your journey in life.

Genealogical Regression Options

As you've already recognized from our earlier exercises, the entire journey you have and the outcome you receive depend on who shows up. That is determined by the intentions you set for which parental figure you want to work on at the time. Once you decide who you would like to meet in your inner world, you have options for what you can work to heal.

Two Options for Insight and Healing

What kinds of things can you heal using this method? The possibilities are endless and unlimited. That won't help us in healing though, so for that reason, I give you two options and two Genealogical Regressions in this chapter. They include challenging issues and the soul's purpose and the lighter nature of living.

Challenging Issues

Most of the time during the Genealogical Regression, the issues that come up involve challenges and difficulties that happened to ancestors. Because the possibilities for how those show up are unlimited, I will review a few of the most common challenges you may uncover during your journey.

- **War**—Experiencing scenes on battlefields is incredibly common during the Genealogical Regression. Obviously, the pains of continual warfare have plagued humankind and left deep scars on the spiritual, emotional, and even physical energetic blueprints for society. When you can travel into the past and send light to these heavy events, you can shift the collective for the benefit of all people worldwide.
- **Death**—Likewise, there are too many sad scenes of funerals or deathbeds in the Genealogical Regression to be understated. Losing those we love hurts, and those hurts can often imprint on the souls of all members of a family line.

- **Illness**—When a family member or ancestor experiences illness either themselves or when they become a caregiver of someone they love, those painful conditions also leave their mark on the DNA and imprint into the soul of those who follow. You may find yourself discovering areas where you can send healing light to ancestors to relieve their pains from illness.

- **Emotional healing and support**—Pain is not always physical. There could be a wide array of scenarios where you feel your ancestor simply needs to experience the feeling of being unconditionally loved or supported, and you can be the loving presence who shows up for them and offers support.

These topics sound quite daunting, I know, but in the sacred space, you and your guide float over events and observe them in a similar fashion to watching a movie or video, so you can do so at a distance and send light to all involved, often making instant shifts in the heavier energies you may encounter.

Soul's Purpose and the Lighter Nature of Living

Our ancestors struggled in many ways, yet that is not to say they didn't experience love, joy, and happiness. Those positive attributes and qualities can be accessed during the Genealogical Regression so you can more fully incorporate them into your daily life. I will review some of the more common examples.

- **Soul's purpose**—I've talked about our soul's purpose for years in other contexts, including discovering our purpose and seeing how it can be repeated during our many past lives. What if your purpose in life is brought forward through your DNA and manifests itself as an inkling for a particular kind of work or calling? It's possible. Discovering these pearls of wisdom can help you bring them forward more fully in your daily life.

- **Talents**—You may be attracted to a certain hobby, such as playing a particular musical instrument or doing arts and crafts. You may have a gift for public speaking or nurturing others. What if, again, this urging is not only from the callings of your own soul, but originates in some early time through your ancestors? You can discover the ancestral source and incorporate your insights into your exploration.

- **Family legacy**—Your family may have wonderful qualities that you will want to experience through the spiritual journey work you can do in the Genealogical Regression. Learning about these gifts will help you appreciate where you come from at a deeper level. You will understand your roots and proudly embody those qualities as you move down the road of life.

- **Recreation and enjoyment**—Did you know some of the recreational activities you enjoy may be things your ancestors did in the past? Explore happy and lighter moments within your family to bring lightness to the gravity of the material world and experience more joy in knowing and understanding the things you have in common with your forebears.

Most of my client sessions explore the heavier side of things, but that might be because there was no active intention to explore happier topics. That's why we will do two Genealogical Regressions so you can consciously notice the lighter side of life regarding your family. If you look and ask, you will find positive things to observe, and doing so can help you relieve the heavy burden you may feel doing the healing work on behalf of your ancestors. Nothing is ever all bad or all good. Let's notice some of the good.

Be Open to Surprises

Keep in mind that in guided imagery, thanks to the power of your own subconscious mind and Higher Self as well as to the support and influences of your ancestors and special guide, anything is possible. You may be in for some surprises. For example, let's say you intended to do a healing with your mother's side of the family. You were raised by your grandparents, and you had in mind the idea of working specifically with your grandmother who raised you. Once you get into the journey, however, what will you do if your mom shows up instead, even though you haven't seen her since childhood? Or what if you were adopted and your birth mother who you don't know at all shows up? What if your dad shows up instead of your mom? The possibilities are endless. Be open and know that whoever appears will be for your highest good.

Be Open to Insights and Intuition

Remember to listen to and trust your inner guidance. I simply cannot stress this enough. Trust what you receive. I recently heard a powerful story from one of my students that is a wonderful reminder to us all about the power of our own intuition. For privacy and to hide her identity, I am paraphrasing this story a bit. Here's what happened. The student took my class, and during guided imagery, she heard a specific name in her mind that she'd never heard before. After the class, the name persisted in her mind. She went to an ancestry website and, lo and behold, she discovered that name belonged to one of her actual ancestors who she had never heard of before. Incredible! I love this story. This is a great reminder to pay attention and not just brush off strange thoughts that come into your mind. They likely mean something, and those ideas would not be coming into your mind if they weren't important.

That is one of the fascinating advantages of doing Ancestral Healing. Should you choose to follow up on your inner work in that way, you just might be able to find real family members who you met in your inner mind and deepen the impact your work is having on yourself and your family.

The bottom line is this: whatever happens, just go with it. Trust yourself. Know that at any given time, we may not get what we want, but we always get what we need. We can set all the intentions we want, but at the end of the day, allowing the highest good to emerge is always best. If unexpected scenarios bubble up, or if someone shows up in your journey who you did not expect, know that the highest good is unfolding. Go with the flow and know that you can always take these journeys again anytime to explore all the many possibilities available.

Genealogical Regression to
Soul's Purpose and the Lighter Nature of Living

With all these ideas in mind, it's time to take your first Genealogical Regression. Based on all the work you've done so far, you will go back into your sacred space, connect with your guide and the parent who shows up, and then you will travel into the past of your ancestors to a time that is most in need of healing. Earlier we discussed that those challenging issues might include death, wars, battles, illnesses, and so forth, but again, be open to discover what you need to rather than being attached to any preconceived notion or outcome.

Remember that you could choose which parent you want to work with in advance, or during the journey, you could simply wait and see who shows up. Since the journey is designed to be reused, you can always go back later to eventually address other possibilities. Recording this exercise in advance will help you go deeper into the practice.

• • ● • •
EXERCISE
Genealogical Regression to
Soul's Purpose and the Lighter Nature of Living

Sit in a comfortable chair with your hands in your lap and feet flat on the floor. Close your eyes. Breathe. Take a deep, healing breath in through your nose, breathing in love and peace and light. Exhale tensions and concerns.

Imagine a beautiful beam of pure white light coming down through the top of your head. Feel that light moving through your head and forehead, floating into your eyes, your nose, your mouth, and your jaw, moving down, down, down, into your neck and shoulders, into your arms, your elbows, your wrists, your hands and fingertips.

Feel the light as it continues flowing down, down, down through your shoulders, flowing down your spine into your heart center. Feel your heart energy expand as the light continues to move down into your stomach, through your torso to the base of your spine, and into your legs, flowing into your thighs, your knees, your calves, your ankles and heels and down into the soles of your feet and into your toes.

Imagine the light is getting stronger now as it flows from your head, through your body, and into your legs and feet. The light begins to pour out of your heart center, creating a beautiful golden ball of light that surrounds you by about three feet in all directions. Feel yourself floating inside this peaceful golden ball of light, and know that within this golden light, only that which is of your highest good can come through.

Imagine a doorway in front of you. You can see the door, feel the door, or just have an inner knowing the door is there. When you count back from three, you will walk through that door and go inside your sacred space where you feel totally relaxed, nurtured, and protected. Ready? Three, two, one; you're opening the door. Open the door now. Walk or float inside your beautiful room. Be there now.

Take a moment to absorb the wonderful feelings of peace and harmony. Allow this place to fill your body with loving light and healing energy.

Pause here.

As you continue to enjoy your sacred space, your loving guide floats down to join you. Imagine they are with you right now. Feel the unconditional love they have for you.

Take a moment now to discuss your intentions for today. Let your guide know that you would like to meet with one of your parents to have an important conversation to discover more details about your soul's purpose, hidden talents, your family legacy, or whatever you feel is for your highest good that would shed light on the positive gifts your ancestors bring to you. If you know which parent and which ancestral line you want to explore, let them know that also. Take your time to discuss all you need.

Pause here.

Once you finish speaking with your guide, notice there's a door on the other side of your room. That door is opening now, and here comes one of your parents. Remember this is their Higher Self, the soul essence of your parent. Notice them now. Who is this? Notice the first thought that comes into your mind. Feel the essence of their soul and notice how happy your parent is to see you.

Imagine you can let your parent know that you would like to visit a positive event within the family history. Take your time to explain this to your parent and imagine they and your guide can assist you in knowing which event is best. Let them both know you want to visit the event that is most in need of healing at this moment, the event that would make the most positive impact on your entire lineage. This may be something that demonstrates your soul's purpose that is common within your ancestry; it may help you reveal a gift or talent or some incident that would reveal the legacy of your entire lineage. Receive clarity about which side of your parent's family you are going to visit today.

Pause here.

As you mention this, imagine you and your parent can take your guide by the hand, and the three of you begin to float toward that door your parent came through. In just a moment, when you count to three, the door will open, and you and your guide and your parent will float through that door, and you will find yourselves traveling in the clouds, floating out over a ray of sunshine that represents your ancestral history. On the count of three, you will open that door. Ready? One, two, and three; you're opening that door now.

Float through the door and be there now, floating in the clouds over a ray of sunshine. Know that this healing sunbeam represents time and your ancestral history. Imagine you are floating over today, and the ray of sunshine stretches on for as far as your eye can see. Know that the farther out you float, the earlier the time will be. Allow your guide to take you and your parent to a very early time in your ancestral history, the time that will be for your highest good at this moment.

Know that today, you, your parent, and your guide are going back in time to a moment in your ancestor's past that will best help you recognize an aspect of your soul's purpose, a talent or gift you can better utilize in your current lifetime and on behalf of your entire family.

The three of you will begin to float. Ready? Floating out, out, out, over the ray of sunshine, you're floating farther and farther and farther, out, out, out to a very early time that will be most for your highest good. Know that the farther out you float, the earlier the time will be.

You're floating way, way, way back to this very early event in your lineage that will give you the most insights into what you are seeking today and what your parent and your guide believe will be most for your and your family's highest good.

On the count of three, you will arrive. Ready? One, floating out, out, out; two, farther and farther, you're almost there; and three, you're there. Be there now, floating over this important time in your ancestral history.

Imagine you and your parent and your guide can float down, down, down, down, down, and hover over these events. Be there now and notice what's happening.

What year is this? Notice the first thought that pops into your mind. Where are you in the world? Again, notice your first thoughts. What's happening? Which ancestor or ancestors do you see? Imagine you can easily sense or feel the energy of your ancestors. Take your time to notice all you can about exactly what is going on and what is happening to your ancestor(s).

Pause here.

How do these events relate to your own soul's purpose or to talents or gifts you inherited from your ancestors? How does this reflect your family legacy and lineage? If needed, imagine you can fast-forward through these events to the situation most in need of recognition and acknowledgment today.

Pause here.

Imagine there is a beautiful healing light coming down from above. This loving light is pouring over this event and sending a loving high frequency to your ancestors and all who are involved in this event. Imagine this loving light is encouraging, supportive, and uplifting. Send this light for as long as you would like, allowing everyone to benefit from this extra love and encouragement. Know that your ancestors and everyone involved in these events are now receiving your intention of unconditional love and healing.

Imagine you and your parent can also receive this loving light and both of you are getting lighter and lighter, brighter and brighter.

As you continue to observe these events, what gifts and talents are being revealed? How do these events and happenings relate to your soul's purpose that may or may not be shared with your entire lineage and family? How do these events represent the legacy of your entire family?

As you all continue to receive this healing, imagine you and your parent can ask your loving guide to explain the lessons you and your family learned from this experience. Take your time and receive all the details you need as you continue to receive this healing light.

Pause here.

Continue to process this information as you, your parent, and your guide continue to send healing light to this very early time in your ancestral history.

Imagine you and your parent and your guide can lift up, up, up, out of these early events, floating higher and higher and higher into the clouds. Imagine you can send a loving healing light to all events and all ancestors in this early time. When you're ready, float back toward today and continue to send healing to every event between those early times and today. Imagine this healing and new knowledge assists and inspires everyone in your family tree from the earliest times through the present day and will continue to benefit those future ancestors who have yet to be born.

As the knowledge of your gifts and this healing light pour into your ray of sunshine, that light now shines brighter and brighter and lighter and lighter than ever before. Float toward today. Continue floating toward today, floating farther and farther and farther, forward in time, allowing all events between this very early time in your lineage and today to totally realign in light of this new knowledge and understanding.

In a moment, when you count back from three, you will once again be floating over today. Ready? Three, two, and one, you're back. Float back through the door you came through. Close that door behind you and go back into your beautiful room and sacred space. Be there now, back inside your sacred space.

Take a moment to speak with your parent and your guide about anything else of importance. Take your time.

Pause here.

Thank your parent for joining you today. Once again feel the unconditional love they have for you at a soul level. Take a moment to talk about anything else of importance.

Pause here.

When you're ready, say goodbye and imagine your parent will walk or float back through the door they first came through earlier.

Take a moment to ask your guide for any further clarity you need about this healing.

Pause here.

When you're finished, thank your loving guide for being here today. Say goodbye for now and watch your guide float back to where they came from. Know you will see your guide again soon.

Take a deep breath in through your nose and allow yourself to become completely relaxed inside your sacred space. Allow the supportive energies of your sacred space to move through every single cell of your being. As you do, breathe in the energy of joy, peace, and happiness as you inhale one, two, three, four, and exhale love and light, one, two, three, four. Very good.

Filled with peaceful light, feeling better than you did before, turn around now and walk back through the door you came through. Close the door behind you and go back out to where you began your journey. Be there now, back where you began.

In a moment, when you count from five, you will come back into the room, feeling awake, refreshed, and better than you felt before.

Five—grounded, centered, and balanced. Four—continuing to process this new energy in your dreams tonight so by tomorrow morning, you will be fully integrated into these new insights. Three—still surrounded by that beautiful golden ball of light, safe and protected, you know that only that which is of your highest good can come through. You will drive carefully and be safe in all activities. Two—you're grounded, centered, and balanced, and one—you're back.

•• • ••

JOURNAL PROMPT
Genealogical Regression to
Soul's Purpose and the Lighter Nature of Living

Take some time to note all the valuable information you received today. Here are a few suggestions for things you may want to write down.

1. Which parental figure met you today?
2. Where did you travel?
3. What year was it and where did this happen?
4. What gifts or talents did you discover that relate to your family legacy and soul's purpose?

5. Did you find commonality between yourself and your lineage? How can that knowing help you in the future?

Remember to take the journey again to work with different ancestors, or if you need more time visiting the people you met today, you can always go visit them again to gain new insights. Be sure to write down any other thoughts that might come in over the course of the next few days or even in your dreams.

By engaging more fully with the heritage and talents brought to you from your ancestors, you can expand your awareness and capabilities to bring greater abundance and joy into your current life and share that energy with future generations of your family.

Genealogical Regression to Heal Challenging Issues

Once you've experienced what the Genealogical Regression is like by tuning in to pleasant happenings within your family tree and ancestral heritage, you can take a much longer Genealogical Regression. This time, knowing you are surrounded by love and light, you will travel into the past to heal a challenging issue or situation that happened with your ancestors. Earlier we discussed a few possibilities of what those issues might be, including death, wars, battles, illnesses, and so forth, but again, be open to discover what you need to rather than being attached to any preconceived notion. Your guide will be with you all the way to help you send transformative, loving light and healing to all involved. Because this journey is far longer than many of the others in the book, recording it in advance will help you tremendously.

•• • ••
EXERCISE
Genealogical Regression to Heal Challenging Issues

Sit in your comfortable sacred space where you do all your healing work. Settle in comfortably and surround yourself with items you love. Sit peacefully with your hands in your lap and feet flat on the floor. Close your eyes. Breathe. Take a deep, healing breath in through your nose, breathing in love and peace and light. Exhale tensions and concerns.

Feel the beautiful beam of pure white light moving down through the top of your head. Feel the light as it continues flowing down, down, down through your entire body—your shoulders, arms, and hands. Allow the light to continue flowing down your spine into your heart center. Feel your heart energy expand as the light continues to move down into your stomach, through your torso to the base of your spine, and into your legs, flowing into your thighs, your knees, your calves, your ankles and heels, and down into the soles of your feet and into your toes.

This loving light is getting stronger now and it begins to pour out of your heart center, creating a beautiful golden ball of light that surrounds you by about three feet in all directions. Feel yourself floating inside this peaceful golden ball of light, and know that within this golden light, only that which is of your highest good can come through.

Notice the door that leads into your beautiful room, your sacred space where you feel totally at ease. Walk through the door now and be inside your sacred space. Be there now.

Take a moment to fill your body with loving light and healing energy. As you do, imagine your loving guide floats down to join you. Feel the love they have for you.

Take a moment now to discuss your intentions for today. Let your guide know you would like to meet with one of your parents to have an important conversation about challenging events that affected your family line—which may include wars, deaths, illnesses, or whatever you feel is for your highest good—that would shed light on the events and situations that most need to be healed at this time. If you know which parent and which ancestral line you want to explore, let them know that also. Take your time to discuss all you need.

Pause here.

Once you finish speaking with your guide, notice there's a door on the other side of your room. That door is opening now, and here comes one of your parents. Remember this is their Higher Self, the soul essence of your parent. Notice them now. Who is this? Notice the first thought that comes into your mind. Feel the essence of their soul and notice how happy your parent is to see you.

Imagine you can let your parent know that you would like to help send healing light to a challenging event that affected the family. This could be a war, a battle, illnesses, or some other event. Take your time to explain this to your parent and imagine they and your guide can assist you in knowing which event is best. Let them both know you want to visit the event that is most in need of healing at this moment, the event that would make the most positive impact on your entire lineage. Receive clarity about which side of your parent's family you are going to visit today.

Pause here.

As you mention this, imagine you and your parent can take your guide by the hand and the three of you begin to float toward that door your parent came through. In just a moment, when you count to three, the door will open, and you and your guide and your parent will float through that door and you will find yourselves traveling in the clouds, floating out over a ray of sunshine that represents your ancestral history. On the count of one, you will open that door. Ready? Three, two, and one; you're opening that door now.

Float through the door and be there now, floating in the clouds over a ray of sunshine. Know that this healing sunbeam represents time and your ancestral history. Imagine you are floating over today, and the ray of sunshine stretches on as far as you can see. Know that the farther out you float, the earlier the time will be. Allow your guide to take you and your parent to a very early time in your ancestral history, the time that will be for your highest good.

Know that today, you, your parent, and your guide are going back in time to a moment in your ancestor's past that would best help you heal a challenging situation that affected your entire lineage. You will travel back to provide healing light that will be of benefit to all in your lineage who will assist you in moving forward now and in the future in the best way possible.

The three of you will begin now to float. Ready? Floating out, out, out, over the ray of sunshine, you're floating farther and farther and farther, out, out, out to a very early time that will be most for your highest good. Know that the farther out you float, the earlier the time will be.

You're floating way, way, way back, to this very early event in your lineage that will give you the most insights into what you are seeking today and what your parent and your guide believe will be most for your and your family's highest good.

On the count of three you will arrive. Ready? One, floating out, out, out; two, farther and farther, you're almost there; and three, you're there. Be there now, floating over this important time in your ancestral history.

Imagine you and your parent and your guide can float down, down, down, down, down, and hover over these events. Remember you are still surrounded by a protective shield of golden light. Within the light you are safe and protected and able to view these events easily. Be there now and notice what's happening.

What year is this? Notice the first thought that pops into your mind. Where are you in the world? Again, notice your first thoughts. What's happening? Which ancestor or ancestors do you see? Imagine you can easily sense or feel the energy of your ancestors. Take your time to notice all you can about exactly what is going on and what is happening to your ancestor.

Pause here.

How do these events reflect your intention today to send light to a troubling or challenging event? Take a moment to notice how your ancestor feels there and how that may be affecting your entire lineage. If needed, imagine you can fast-forward through these events to the situation most in need of healing today.

Pause here.

Imagine there is a beautiful healing light coming down from above. This loving light is pouring over this event and sending a loving high frequency to your ancestors and all who are involved in this event. Imagine this energy is getting lighter and lighter and lighter, brighter and brighter and brighter. Allow your loving light to raise the vibrations and frequencies around these challenging events. Imagine you, your parent, and your guide can easily send this light for as long as you would like.

Pause here.

As you continue to send the loving light, you notice the heavy energy surrounding these events begins to feel more peaceful than before. Your intentions and this light are calming the energy and this situation is becoming better than before, even if that improvement is only slight. Take your time as you begin to perceive these shifts taking place.

Pause here.

Know you are making an impact by sending this loving healing light. Surround everyone there in unconditional love and healing. Imagine now that the light you, your parent, and your guide are sending is making an incredible impact on everyone. As you notice that energy, you can also see that there is an energetic cord of light connecting you and your parent to this very early event. These light cords are coming out of your stomach or solar plexus areas and connecting you with these ancestors and the events below you.

Your guide is now holding a big pair of golden scissors. In a moment, when you count from three, your guide will cut the cords between you and your parent and these very early ancestors and events. Ready? Three, two, one; your guide is cutting the cords now.

As these cords are cut, you notice the light pouring down from above now moves through you and your parent and both of you are getting lighter and lighter and lighter and brighter and brighter and brighter. That healing light extends now to all the family members in your lineage as your entire family becomes lighter and brighter, lighter than ever before.

Take a moment while this healing energy refreshes you and notice how much better you feel. Notice how much lighter and brighter your parent looks and feels.

As you continue to receive this healing, imagine you and your parent can ask your loving guide to explain the lessons you and your family learned from this experience. Take your time and receive all the details you need as you continue to receive this healing light.

Pause here.

Continue to process this information as you, your parent, and your guide continue to send healing light to this very early time in your ancestral history.

Imagine you and your parent and your guide can lift up, up, up, out of these early events, floating higher and higher and higher into the clouds. Hold hands with your parent and guide and the three of you will begin to float back toward today, but only as quickly as you can send that loving healing light to all events and all ancestors between these early times and today. Imagine this healing light pours into your ray of sunshine, making that light shine brighter and brighter and lighter and lighter than ever before. Float toward today now. Floating farther and farther, forward in time, allowing all events to heal and transform now. Continue floating toward today, allowing all events between that very early event and today to totally realign in light of this new understanding and healing.

When you count back from three, you will be back, floating over today. Ready? Three, two, and one; you're back. Float back through the door you came through. Close that door behind you and go back into your beautiful room and sacred space. Be there now, back inside your sacred space.

Take a moment to speak with your parent and your guide about anything else of importance. Take your time.

Pause here.

Thank your parent for joining you today. Once again feel the unconditional love they have for you at a soul level. Take a moment to talk about anything else of importance.

Pause here.

When you're ready, say goodbye and imagine your parent will walk or float back through the door they first came through.

Take a moment to ask your guide for any further clarity you need about this healing.

Pause here.

When you're finished, thank your loving guide for being here today. Say goodbye for now and watch your guide float back to where they came from. Know you will see your guide again soon.

Take a deep breath in through your nose and allow yourself to become completely relaxed inside your sacred space. Allow the supportive energies of your sacred space to move through every single cell of your being. As you do, breathe in the energy of joy, peace, and happiness as you inhale one, two, three, four, and exhale love and light, one, two, three, four. Very good.

Filled with peaceful light, feeling better than you did before, turn around now and walk back through the door you came through. Close the door behind you and go back out to where you began your journey. Be there now, back where you began.

In a moment, when you count from five, you will come back into the room, feeling awake, refreshed, and better than you felt before.

Five—grounded, centered, and balanced. Four—continuing to process this new energy in your dreams tonight so by tomorrow morning, you will be fully integrated into these new insights. Three—still surrounded by that beautiful golden ball of light, safe and protected, you know that only that which is of your highest good can come through. You will drive carefully and be safe in all activities. Two—you're grounded, centered, and balanced, and one—you're back.

•• ● ••

JOURNAL PROMPT
Genealogical Regression to Heal Challenging Issues

Take a moment to reflect on all you learned.

1. Which parent met with you today?

2. Where did you travel to and what year did you visit?

3. Describe the challenging issue in detail. Make note of anything you remembered that felt important to recall.

4. How did those difficult events affect the entire family line? Your parent? You directly?

5. What lessons did the family learn from these events?

6. How can this new light and healing help the family move forward in the future?

7. How did you feel after sending the healing light to your ancestor and others? Did you feel better as a result? If so, how?

There is much to uncover with this journey, so be sure and keep your journal handy for the next days and perhaps even weeks in case new insights emerge. The journey may bring up tremendous emotion as you experience the plight of your ancestors. If so, tread lightly and process this information in any way that supports you. A nice walk may be good, or a trip to a store you love—anything that makes you feel at ease and happy is good to do. Whenever you feel you want to learn more about the ancestors you encountered today, remember you can use this journey for other parents and other situations in any of your family lines.

Summing Up

Sending this needed light to challenging situations goes to the very heart of this work. When you invest today in lightening things for your ancestors in the past, the future will be brighter for everyone. Amazing job and congratulations. You should be proud of yourself for taking the time to go through these important journeys. They not only benefit you and your family, but all sentient beings from the past, present, and future. When we all work as a collective to shift consciousness, we can move forward into a brighter and empowered tomorrow.

CHAPTER FIVE

Ancestral Past-Life Regressions

One of the best ways to understand your relationship with your immediate family is by discovering how you've known different family members or caregivers in prior incarnations. The incredible bond and commitment we make when our souls choose to align with our family is so profound, it's likely that you have lived with at least some of these individuals in other times and places. As mentioned throughout this book, the family does not have to be blood related. The family could include the same varied caregivers discussed earlier—foster parents, grandparents, aunts and uncles, and the like. You meet familiar people throughout your journey in life who you knew in the past and who you come into this life to meet again to learn lessons and love. It makes sense that the family members who are so close to us are often familiar people from times long gone. You will explore more about these important connections through several guided journeys in this chapter. Because all these exercises are more involved and longer than many of the others, I highly recommend you record the ones you choose to do up front so you can relax and get the most out of the journeys.

Discovering Past Lives with Your Parental Figure

In this upcoming journey, you will go back into the same space as before, only this time, your guide will help you discover past-life links with the parental figure you are going to inquire about. For simplicity,

I will refer to this person as your parent. Remember that you set the intention for who you want to meet in your inner world. Later, you can redo this journey to discover your links with your other parent. You can also take the regression more than once with the same parent to discover more past lives.

We've talked all about what it means to be a parent and the numerous iterations of parent, from the person who gave birth to you, to an adoptive parent or foster parent, and so forth. Knowing the connection that you share with any of these parents is important and helpful and can assist you in getting along better in your current incarnation.

•• ● ••
EXERCISE
Discovering Past Lives with Your Parental Figure

Sit in a comfortable chair with your hands in your lap and feet flat on the floor. Close your eyes. Breathe. Take a deep, healing breath in through your nose, breathing in love and peace and light. Exhale tensions and concerns.

Imagine a beautiful beam of pure white light coming down through the top of your head. Feel that light moving through your head and forehead, floating into your eyes, your nose, your mouth, and your jaw, moving down, down, down, into your neck and shoulders, into your arms, your elbows, your wrists, your hands and fingertips.

Feel the light as it continues flowing down, down, down through your shoulders, flowing down your spine into your heart center. Feel your heart energy expand as the light continues to move down into your stomach, through your torso to the base of your spine, and into your legs, flowing into your thighs, your knees, your calves, your ankles and heels, and down into the soles of your feet and into your toes.

Imagine the light is getting stronger now as it flows from your head, through your body, and into your legs and feet. The light begins to pour out of your heart center, creating a beautiful golden ball of light that surrounds you by about three feet in all directions. Feel yourself floating inside this peaceful golden ball of light, and know that within this golden light, only that which is of your highest good can come through.

Imagine there's a doorway in front of you. You can see the door, feel the door, or just have an inner knowing the door is there. When you count back from three, you will walk through that door and go inside your sacred space where you feel totally relaxed, nurtured, and protected. Ready? Three, two, one; you're opening the door. Walk or float inside your beautiful room. Be there now.

Take a moment to absorb the wonderful feelings of peace and harmony. Allow this place to fill your body with loving light and healing energy.

Pause here.

As you continue to enjoy your sacred space, imagine your loving guide floats down to join you. Imagine they are with you right now. Feel the unconditional love they have for you.

Take a moment to discuss your intentions for today. Let your guide know you would like to meet with one of your parental figures to discover where and when you knew each other in past lives. If you know which parent and which ancestral line you want to explore, let your guide know that also. Take your time to discuss all you need.

Pause here.

Once you finish speaking with your guide, notice there's a door on the other side of your room. That door is opening now, and here comes one of your parents. Remember this is their Higher Self, the soul essence of your parent. Notice them now. Who is this? Notice the first thought that comes into your mind. Feel the essence of their soul and notice how happy your parent is to see you.

Imagine you can let your parent know that you would like to explore your shared past lives. Take your time to discuss this with your parent and guide. Remember that because your guide has known your soul since the beginning of time, your guide can assist you in finding the time that would be most for your highest good.

Pause here.

As you continue to discuss this, imagine you and your parent can take your guide by the hand and the three of you begin now to float. You're lifting off the ground, floating higher and higher and higher, up, up, up and into the clouds. Imagine that the higher up you float, the more relaxed you feel. Continuing to soar into the clouds, floating up, up, up, higher and higher, more and more relaxed. Traveling peacefully into the clouds, imagine you have floated so high in the sky that you look down and notice you are now floating over a ray of sunshine. That ray of sunshine represents your soul's history. Gaze out now in the direction of your soul's past. Notice how bright your past is. Turn now toward the opposite direction and look into your future. Notice how bright your future is.

As you continue to float over today, turn again and notice the direction of your past. As you do, notice the past is getting lighter and lighter and lighter, brighter and brighter than before. You can also notice that the ray of sunshine stretches into the past for as far as your eye can see.

With your guide and parent with you, float over today and ask your guide an important question: Did I know my parent in past lives? Notice the first thought that pops into your mind.

If the answer is no, you will continue your journey today by visiting one of your parent's most influential past lives, a lifetime that will be for your highest good to know about and understand. If the answer is yes, then in just a moment, your guide will take you and your parent back into the past to the most significant lifetime the two of you shared, or to one that will be most for your highest good at this moment in time.

Take your guide and your parent by the hands now and the three of you will begin to float. Know that the farther out you float, the earlier the time will be. Allow your guide to take you and your parent to a very early time in your soul's history, to a time that will be most for your highest good.

The three of you will begin to float now. Ready? Floating out, out, out, over the ray of sunshine, you're floating farther and farther and farther into the past, out, out, out to a very early time that will be most for your highest good. You're floating way, way, way back, to this very early event in your soul's history that will give you the most insight into what you are seeking today and what your parent and your guide believe will be most for your highest good.

On the count of three, you will arrive. Ready? One, floating out, out, out; two, farther and farther, you're almost there; and three, you're there. Be there now, floating over this important event.

Imagine you, your parent, and your guide can float down, down, down, down, down, into these events. Be there now and notice what's happening.

What year is this? Notice the first thought that pops into your mind. Where are you in the world? Again, notice your first thoughts. What's happening? Are you alone or with other people? Imagine you can fast-forward through these events to a moment when you and your parent are together. Be there now. Notice what's happening.

What kind of relationship did you and your parent have in this early time? How does the relationship reflect what you're doing together in your current lifetime? Take your time to notice all you can about exactly what is going on and what is happening between the two of you.

Pause here.

What lessons are your souls learning about in this very early time? How do those lessons relate to your current life? What agreements did your souls make about being together? Discover and notice any other important details about the connection between you and your parent. Take your time.

Pause here.

Imagine there is a beautiful healing light coming down from above. This loving light is pouring over this lifetime you shared with your parent. Your guide is sending a loving high-frequency light to you, your parent, and all who are in this life with you. Imagine this loving light is encouraging, supportive, and uplifting. Allow your guide to send this light for as long as you would like, allowing everyone to benefit from this extra love and encouragement. Know that everyone involved is now receiving your intention of unconditional love and healing that you, your guide, and your parent are sending today. Both you and your parent easily receive this loving light and both of you are getting lighter and lighter, brighter and brighter.

Pause here.

Continue to process this information as you, your parent, and your guide lift up, up, up, out of these early events, floating higher and higher and higher into the clouds. Continue to send love and light to all people who lived in that early time. The healing light pours into your ray of sunshine, and that light now shines brighter and brighter and lighter and lighter than ever before. Float toward today now. Continue floating toward today, forward in time, allowing all events between this very early time and today to totally realign in light of this new knowledge and understanding.

In a moment, when you count back from three, you will once again be floating over today. Ready? Three, two, and one; you're back. Still holding your parent and guide by the hand, imagine the three of you can float down, down, down, back through the clouds until you land inside your beautiful room. Be there now, inside your beautiful sacred space. Take a moment to speak with your parent and your guide about anything else of importance. Take your time.

Pause here.

Thank your parent for joining you today. Feel the unconditional love they have for you at a soul level. Take a moment to talk about anything else of importance.

Pause here.

When you're ready, say goodbye and imagine your parent will walk or float back through the door they first came through earlier.

Take a moment to ask your guide for any further clarity you need about this healing.

Pause here.

When you're finished, thank your loving guide for being here today. Say goodbye for now and watch your guide float back to where they came from. Know that you will see your guide again soon.

Take a deep breath in through your nose and allow yourself to become completely relaxed inside your sacred space. Allow the supportive energies of your sacred space to move through every single cell of your being. As you do, breathe in the energy of joy, peace, and happiness as you inhale, and exhale love and light. Very good.

Filled with peaceful light, feeling better than you did before, turn around now and walk back through the door you came through. Close the door behind you and go back out to where you began your journey. Be there now, back where you began.

In a moment, when you count from five, you will come back into the room, feeling awake, refreshed, and better than you felt before.

Five—grounded, centered, and balanced. Four—continuing to process this new energy in your dreams tonight so by tomorrow morning, you will be fully integrated into these new insights. Three—still surrounded by that beautiful golden ball of light, safe and protected, you know that only that which is of your highest good can come through. You will drive carefully and be safe in all activities. Two—you're grounded, centered, and balanced, and one—you're back.

•• ● ••

JOURNAL PROMPT
Discovering Past Lives with Your Parental Figure

Take some time to make note of all the valuable information you received today. Here are a few suggestions for things you may want to write down.

1. Which parent met with you today?
2. Did you have a past life together?

3. Where did you travel?

4. What year did you visit?

5. How did the experiences of that early time influence your soul connection in your present lifetime?

Always feel free to expand and describe anything important you want to remember later. You can also use the journey again to discover more past lives you shared with the parent who showed up this time and to address other parents or parental figures by simply shifting your intentions.

Understanding Your Parental Figure's Important Past Lives

One of the big breakthroughs I experienced that led to writing this book involved a clear inner vision of who my parents had been in previous lifetimes. This is different from the exercise you just went through because there are obviously many lifetimes you and your parents didn't share. Understanding and identifying your parent or parental figure's most *influential* past lives, whether you were in them or not, helps you know more about the subconscious forces and influences that affect them in their current lifetime. By *influential*, I mean the lifetime and behaviors that are coming through them the most in their current incarnation. When you think about it, because we've all had so many different soul experiences, there may only be a handful of prior experiences that we bring forth into the present at any given time.

The soul strives to develop familiar gifts and talents, embody its purpose, and so forth. Sometimes, souls may even manifest themselves with a similar disposition or personality. Having that knowledge can vastly assist the healing process by opening new avenues of understanding, grace, and empathy toward your parent. Without a doubt, the information can inform you how to better deal with your parents at a soul level so you can get along better.

In this next journey, you will take another past-life regression to discover new insights about the parent of your choice and learn about their past lives that most significantly affect them in the here and now.

•• ● ••
EXERCISE
Understanding Your Parental Figure's Important Past Lives

Retreat to your personal space, close your eyes, and relax. Breathe. Take a deep, healing breath in through your nose, breathing in love and peace and light. Exhale tensions and concerns.

Allow the beautiful beam of pure white light to move through your body from head to feet. As the light becomes ever stronger, feel the light pour forth from your heart center and surround you by about three feet in all directions. Feel yourself floating inside this peaceful golden ball of light, and know that within this golden light, only that which is of your highest good can come through.

Notice the door that leads to your sacred space. When you count from three, you will open that door and return to your beautiful room. Ready? Three, two, one; you're opening the door. Open the door now and walk or float inside your beautiful room. Be there now.

As you enjoy the beneficial vibrations of your sacred space, imagine your loving guide floats down to join you. Imagine they are with you right now. Feel the unconditional love they have for you.

Take a moment now to discuss your intentions for today. Let your guide know which parental figure you would like to meet today. You may also choose to allow the person who is for your highest good to come through and allow your guide to assist you with that. Once that's settled, let your loving guide know that you want to discover your parental figure's most significant past lives. If you know which ancestral line you want to explore, let your guide know that also, or again, allow your highest good to emerge. Take your time to discuss all you need.

Pause here.

Once you finish speaking with your guide, notice there's a door on the other side of your room. That door is opening now, and here comes one of your parental figures. Remember this is their Higher Self, the soul essence of your parental figure. Notice them now. Who is this? Notice the first thought that comes into your mind. Feel the essence of their soul and notice how happy your parent is to see you.

Imagine you can let your parent know that you would like to learn more about their most important and influential past lives. Take your time to discuss this with your parent and guide. Remember that because your guide has known your soul since the beginning of time, your guide can assist you in finding the time that would be most for your highest good.

Pause here.

As you continue to discuss this, imagine you and your parent can take your guide by the hand and the three of you begin now to float. You're lifting off the ground, floating higher and higher and higher, up, up, up and into the clouds. Imagine that the higher up you float, the more relaxed you feel. Continuing to soar into the clouds, floating up, up, up, higher and higher, more and more relaxed. Traveling peacefully into the clouds, imagine you have floated so high in the sky that you are now floating over a ray of sunshine. That ray of sunshine represents your soul's history. Gaze out now in the direction of your soul's past. Notice how bright your past is. Turn toward the opposite direction and look into your future. Notice how bright your future is.

As you continue to float over today, turn again and notice the direction of your past. As you do, notice the past is getting lighter and lighter and lighter, brighter and brighter than before. You can also notice that the ray of sunshine stretches into the past for as far as your eye can see.

With your guide and parent with you, float over today and ask your guide to help you by taking you to one of your parent's most influential past lives, a lifetime that will be for your highest good to know about and understand. In just a moment, your guide will take you and your parent back into the past to your parent's most significant lifetime, or to one that will be most for your highest good.

Take your guide and your parent by the hands now and in a moment, the three of you will begin to float. Know that the farther out you float, the earlier the time will be. Allow your guide to take you and your parent to a very early time in your parent's soul's history, to a time that will be most for your highest good at this moment.

The three of you will begin to float now. Ready? Floating out, out, out, over the ray of sunshine, you're floating farther and farther and farther into the past, out, out, out to a very early time that will be most for your highest good. You're floating way, way, way back, to this very early event in your soul's history that will give you the most insight.

On the count of three, you will arrive. Ready? One, floating out, out, out; two, farther and farther, you're almost there; and three, you're there. Be there now, floating over this important event.

Imagine you, your parent, and your guide can float down, down, down, down, down, into these events where you can experience your parent's past life. Be there now and notice what's happening.

What year is this? Notice the first thought that pops into your mind. Where is your parent in the world? Again, notice your first thoughts. What's happening? Are they alone or with other people? Imagine you can fast-forward through these events to a moment where your parent is with other people and notice what's happening.

Pause here.

What lessons did their soul learn about in this very early time? How do those lessons influence their current lifetime? Discover and notice any other important details about how this past life may or may not influence the relationship between you and your parent. Take your time.

Pause here.

Imagine there is a beautiful healing light coming down from above. This loving light is pouring over your parent and this lifetime. Your guide is sending everyone in this lifetime a loving high frequency. Imagine this loving light is encouraging, supportive, and uplifting. Allow your guide to send this light for as long as you would like, allowing everyone to benefit from this energy. Know that everyone involved is now receiving your intention of unconditional love and healing. Your parent easily receives this loving light and becomes lighter and lighter, brighter and brighter.

Pause here.

Continue to process this information as you, your parent, and your guide lift up, up, up, out of these early events, floating higher and higher and higher into the clouds. Hold hands with your parent and guide and the three of you will begin to float back toward today, but only as quickly as you can send that same loving healing light to all events between these early times and today. The healing light pours into your ray of sunshine, and that light now shines brighter and brighter and lighter and lighter than ever before. Float toward today now. Continue floating toward today, floating forward in time, allowing all events between this very early time and today to totally realign in light of this new knowledge and understanding. As you do, you notice your parent continuing to become lighter and brighter than ever before.

In a moment, when you count back from three, you will once again be floating over today. Ready? Three, two, and one; you're back. Still holding your parent and guide by the hand, imagine the three of you float down, down, down, back through the clouds until you land inside your beautiful room. Be there now, inside your sacred space. Take a moment to speak with your parent and your guide about anything else of importance. Take your time.

Pause here.

Thank your parent for joining you today. Feel the unconditional love they have for you at a soul level. Take a moment to talk about anything else of importance.

Pause here.

When you're ready, say goodbye and imagine your parent will walk or float back through the door they first came through.

Take a moment to ask your guide for any further clarity you need about this healing.

Pause here.

When you're finished, thank your loving guide for being here today. Say goodbye for now and watch your guide float back to where they came from. Know that you will see your guide again soon.

Take a deep breath in through your nose and allow yourself to become completely relaxed inside your sacred space. Allow the supportive energies of your sacred space to move through every single cell of your being. As you do, breathe in the energy of joy, peace, and happiness, and exhale love and light. Very good.

Filled with peaceful light, feeling better than you did before, turn around now and walk back through the door you came through. Close the door behind you and go back out to where you began your journey. Be there now, back where you began.

In a moment, when you count from five, you will come back into the room, feeling awake, refreshed, and better than you felt before.

Five—grounded, centered, and balanced. Four—continuing to process this new energy in your dreams tonight so by tomorrow morning, you will be fully integrated into these new insights. Three—still surrounded by that beautiful golden ball of light, safe and protected, you know only that which is of your highest good can come through. You will drive carefully and be safe in all activities. Two—you're grounded, centered, and balanced, and one—you're back.

•• • ••
JOURNAL PROMPT
Understanding Your Parental Figure's Important Past Lives

Take some time to make note of all the valuable information you received today. Here are a few suggestions for things you may want to write down.

1. Which parental figure met with you today?

2. Where did you travel to find their most influential lifetime?

3. What year did you visit?

4. How did that lifetime influence your parental figure's current life?

5. How does this lifetime affect you personally as you relate to your parent?

Because we've all had many lives, you can always return and learn more about the parent you explored today. It's incredibly revealing and helpful to do so. Any parental figure has influences from their prior incarnations, so if you feel guided, use new intentions to continue the exploration with other important souls in your life.

Past-Life Regression to Discover Your Ties to an Ancestor

One interesting exercise to do is to go back to your notes from the earlier chapters and spend some time contemplating some of the ancestors you met there. Once you do that, you can pick someone who you feel a strong connection to and go on a past-life regression to see if the two of you are not only ancestrally linked but knew each other in a past life.

If you don't feel guided to investigate anyone specific, this journey will also allow you to go into the past to an ancestor who you have that prior link with by not being as specific about which ancestor you want to explore.

When you think about how random the universe can be, your unique ancestry is an absolute miracle. Your parents somehow met, and you were born and there is nobody else in this world exactly like you who has both your mother's and father's family lineage combined along with all your own past lives, lessons, and soul purpose.

That's why there are so often more links to the ancestors than to the family bond alone. At a soul level, you chose your family, and this may be in part due to bonds you had in other lifetimes. This journey will give you a chance to find out more.

Prior to starting, you can decide up front to inquire about whatever is for your highest good or you can ask to learn about a specific ancestor. It's entirely your choice. Remember though that you may set your intention and get into the journey and something else may pop up. Just know and trust that the highest and best is working in your life.

•• ● ••

EXERCISE

Past-Life Regression to Discover Your Ties to an Ancestor

Sit in your comfortable space, close your eyes, and relax. Bring the healing white light down from above and allow that loving light to move through every single cell in your body. The light surrounds you now in a golden orb of healing protection. Within the light, you are safe and protected now and always. See, feel, or have an inner knowing about the doorway in front of you that leads to your beautiful room. Open that door now and float inside this special place. Be there now.

Take a moment to absorb the wonderful feelings of peace and harmony. Imagine your loving guide floats down to join you. Imagine they are with you right now. Feel the unconditional love they have for you.

Take a moment to discuss your intentions for today. Let your guide know that you would like to meet with one of your ancestors to discover where and when you knew each other in past lives. If you know which ancestor and which ancestral line you want to explore, let your guide know that also, or you may ask for your highest good. Take your time to discuss all you need.

Pause here.

Once you finish speaking with your guide, notice there's a door on the other side of your room. That door is opening now, and here comes one of your ancestors. Remember this is their Higher Self, the soul essence of your ancestor. Notice them now. Who is this? Notice the first thought that comes into your mind. Feel the essence of their soul and notice how happy your ancestor is to see you. Take a moment here to allow them to fully introduce themselves and feel free to ask them anything you'd like.

Pause here.

Imagine you can let your ancestor know that you would like to explore your shared past lives. Take your time to discuss this with your ancestor and guide. Remember that because your guide has known your soul since the beginning of time, your guide can assist you in finding the time that would be most for your highest good.

Pause here.

As you continue to discuss this, imagine you and your ancestor can take your guide by the hand and the three of you begin to float. You're lifting off the ground, floating higher and higher and higher, up, up, up and into the clouds. Imagine that the higher up you float, the more relaxed you feel. Continuing to soar into the clouds, floating up, up, up, higher and higher, more and more relaxed. Traveling peacefully into the clouds, imagine you have floated so high in the sky that you are now floating over a ray of sunshine. That ray of sunshine represents your soul's history. Gaze out now in the direction of your soul's past. Notice how bright your past is. Turn toward the opposite direction and look into your future. Notice how bright your future is.

As you continue to float over today, turn again, and notice the direction of your past. As you do, notice the past is getting lighter and lighter and lighter, brighter and brighter than before. You can also notice the ray of sunshine stretches into the past as far as your eye can see.

With your guide and ancestor with you, float over today and ask your guide an important question: Did I know this ancestor in past lives? Notice the first thought that pops into your mind.

If the answer is no, you will continue your journey today by visiting one of your ancestor's most influential past lives, a lifetime that will be for your highest good to know about and understand. If the answer is yes, then in just a moment, your guide will take you and your ancestor back into the past to the most significant lifetime the two of you shared, or to one that will be most for your highest good at this moment in time.

Take your guide and your ancestor by the hands now and in a moment, the three of you will begin to float. Ready? Floating out, out, out, over the ray of sunshine, you're floating farther and farther and farther into the past, out, out, out to a very early time that will be most for your highest good. You're floating way, way, way back, to this very early event in your soul's history that will give you the most insight into what you are seeking today and what your ancestor and your guide believe will be most for your highest good.

On the count of three, you will arrive. Ready? One, floating out, out, out; two, farther and farther, you're almost there; and three, you're there. Be there now, floating over this important event.

Imagine you, your ancestor, and your guide can float down, down, down, down, down, into these events. Be there now and notice what's happening.

What year is this? Notice the first thought that pops into your mind. Where are you in the world? Again, notice your first thoughts. What's happening? Are you alone or with other people? Imagine you can fast-forward through these events to a moment where you and your ancestor are together. Be there now. Notice what's happening.

What kind of relationship did you and your ancestor have in this early time? How does the relationship from this past life influence your current lifetime? Notice the gifts of this connection and notice any challenges you face because of this past life. Take your time to notice all you can about exactly what is going on and what is happening between the two of you.

Pause here.

What lessons are your souls learning about in this very early time? How do those lessons relate to your current life? What agreements did your souls make about being together? Discover and notice any other important details about the connection between you and your ancestor. Take your time.

Pause here.

Imagine there is a beautiful healing light coming down from above. This loving light is pouring over this lifetime you shared with your ancestor. Your guide is sending everyone a loving high frequency. Imagine this loving light is encouraging, supportive, and uplifting. Allow your guide to send this light for as long as you would like, allowing everyone to benefit from this extra love and encouragement. Know that everyone involved is now receiving your intention of unconditional love and healing. Both you and your ancestor easily receive this loving light and both of you are getting lighter and lighter, brighter and brighter.

If there are any gifts and talents, imagine you can more fully embrace those in your current lifetime. If there are challenging influences, imagine your guide is bringing out a big pair of golden scissors. In a moment, when you count to three, your guide will cut an energetic cord connecting you with the events of this previous lifetime so you will only be influenced by the positive aspects, and you will release any heavier energy. Ready? One, two, and three, cutting that cord now. Feel a beautiful light flowing into your stomach, into your heart, your arms and legs and mind. Allow the light to fill in the space previously occupied by any unwanted influences.

Pause here.

Continue to process this information as you, your ancestor, and your guide lift up, up, up, out of these early events, floating higher and higher and higher into the clouds. Hold hands with your ancestor and guide and imagine the three of you can send loving healing light to everyone who lived in those early times. When you're ready, float back toward the present day, and as you do, send healing and love to all your ancestors who lived between those early times and today. The healing light pours into your ray of sunshine, and that light now shines brighter and brighter and lighter and lighter than ever before. Float toward today now. Continue floating toward today, allowing all events between this very early time and today to totally realign in light of this new knowledge and understanding.

In a moment, when you count back from three, you will once again be floating over today. Ready? Three, two, and one; you're back. Still holding your ancestor and guide by the hand, imagine the three of you can float down, down, down, back through the clouds until you land inside your beautiful room. Be there now, inside your beautiful sacred space. Take a moment to speak with your ancestor and your guide about anything else of importance. Take your time.

Pause here.

Thank your ancestor for joining you today. Feel the unconditional love they have for you at a soul level. Take a moment to talk about anything else of importance.

Pause here.

When you're ready, say goodbye; your ancestor will walk or float back through the door they first came through.

Take a moment to ask your guide for any further clarity you need about this healing.

Pause here.

When you're finished, thank your loving guide for being here today. Say goodbye for now and watch your guide float back to where they came from. Know you will see your guide again soon.

Take a deep breath in through your nose and allow yourself to completely relax inside your sacred space. Allow the supportive energies of your sacred space to move through every single cell of your being. As you do, breathe in the energy of joy, peace, and happiness as you inhale, and exhale love and light. Very good.

Filled with peaceful light, feeling better than you did before, turn around now and walk back through the door you came through. Close the door behind you and go back out to where you began your journey. Be there now, back where you began.

In a moment, when you count from five, you will come back into the room, feeling awake, refreshed, and better than you felt before.

Five—grounded, centered, and balanced. Four—continuing to process this new energy in your dreams tonight so by tomorrow morning, you will be fully integrated into these new insights. Three—still surrounded by that beautiful golden ball of light, safe and protected, you know that only that which is of your highest good can come through. You will drive carefully and be safe in all activities. Two—you're grounded, centered, and balanced, and one—you're back.

•• • ••

JOURNAL PROMPT
Past-Life Regression to Discover Your Ties to an Ancestor

Here are a few suggestions for things you may want to write down about details you uncovered concerning your ancestor.

1. Which ancestor did you meet today?
2. Did you share any past lives together?
3. Where did you travel?
4. What year?
5. Why was the event you visited important to assisting your own journey in your current life?

There are unlimited possibilities for this journey because you have so many ancestors you could explore. Continue to use the recording whenever you feel guided to heal and learn more about your connection to your ancestors, who are all part of your soul agreements and purpose.

Past-Life Regression
to Discover Your Ties to a Living Relative

We all know our families can be a great source of stress. That's one of the best reasons for engaging in Ancestral Healing in the first place, to hopefully smooth out some of the rougher edges around the family bonds. Although we have primarily been working together on your parents, the fun doesn't stop with them. It's highly likely that you have some strong bonds to other members of your family and other people in your life. Even though you're primarily focusing on ancestors in this book, the people you know in your current lifetime—including close friends, enemies, your boss or coworkers, and everyone else you encounter—are often the source of some of the most intense and potentially stressful situations you'll experience during your lifetime. Spending some time learning more about the bonds you have with your living relatives and other important people in your life can help make those situations more tenable. Living relatives could include your siblings, grandparents, aunts, uncles, cousins, and so forth. If you have stepbrothers or sisters, you could also use this journey for them. Although I use the term *living* here, by that I mean people you met in person during your lifetime. It's quite possible that a beloved aunt or uncle, for example, passed away before you were born. The focus here is to learn about people you had a chance to meet, whether they are still on the earth plane or not.

As usual, make at least a preliminary decision about who you want to meet during this journey. Let's say you want to explore a tie you have with one of your sisters to see if you've known each other in past lives. You still may go into the sacred space and find that your brother shows up instead. If that happens, know it's meant to be and go with the flow. Including friends and associates leaves you open for your highest good to emerge since you never know for sure who will appear.

Remember, if the person you expect doesn't appear initially, you can always take the journey again. What comes up will be timely and important for where you're at on your path. In the journey, I call this person your relative, but again, set your intention and know that this could be anyone you choose. The term *relative* refers to anybody you're relating to, so as with all exercises in this book, make this your own.

•• • ••
EXERCISE
Past-Life Regression to
Discover Your Ties to a Living Relative

Sit in your comfortable chair with your hands in your lap and feet flat on the floor. Close your eyes. Breathe. Take a deep, healing breath in through your nose, breathing in love and peace and light. Exhale tensions and concerns.

Imagine a beautiful beam of pure white light coming down through the top of your head. Feel that light moving through your head and forehead, floating into your eyes, your nose, your mouth, and your jaw, moving down, down, down, into your neck and shoulders, into your arms, your elbows, your wrists, your hands and fingertips.

Allow this light to flow down, down through your shoulders, your heart center, your stomach, through your torso to the base of your spine, and into your legs, your thighs, your knees, your calves, your ankles, and heels, and down into the soles of your feet and into your toes.

Imagine the light becomes stronger and begins to pour out of your heart center, creating a beautiful golden ball of light that surrounds you by about three feet in all directions. Feel yourself floating inside this peaceful golden ball of light, and know that within this golden light, only that which is of your highest good can come through.

Notice and walk through your special doorway into your sacred space where you feel totally relaxed, nurtured, and protected. Be there now.

Your loving guide is there waiting for you. Take a moment now to discuss your intentions for today. Let your guide know that you would like to meet with one of your living relatives to discover where and when you knew each other in past lives. If you know which relative you would like to meet with today, let your guide know that or let your guide know you are interested in seeing who shows up, and you understand that either way, the person you meet will provide insights and information that will be for your highest good. Take your time to discuss all you need.

Pause here.

Once you finish speaking with your guide, notice there's a door on the other side of your room. That door is opening now, and here comes one of your relatives. Remember this is their Higher Self, the soul essence of your relative. Notice them now. Who is this? Notice the first thought that comes into your mind. Feel the essence of their soul and notice how happy your relative is to see you.

Remember also that this person may have already crossed into spirit, or they may still be alive. They are someone you know or knew in your current lifetime.

Imagine you can let your relative know that you would like to explore your shared past lives that would be most for your highest good.

Pause here.

As you continue to discuss this, imagine you and your relative can take your guide by the hand and the three of you begin now to float. You're lifting off the ground, floating higher and higher and higher, up, up, up and into the clouds. Imagine that the higher up you float, the more relaxed you feel. Continuing to soar into the clouds, floating up, up, up, higher and higher, more and more relaxed. Traveling peacefully into the clouds, imagine you have floated so high in the sky that you are now floating over a ray of sunshine. That ray of sunshine represents your soul's history. Gaze out now in the direction of your soul's past. Notice how bright your past is. Turn now toward the opposite direction and look into your future. Notice how bright your future is.

As you continue to float over today, turn again and notice the direction of your past. As you do, notice the past is getting lighter and lighter and lighter, brighter and brighter than before. You can also notice that the ray of sunshine stretches into the past as far as your eye can see.

With your guide and relative with you, float over today and ask your guide an important question: Did I know my relative in past lives? Notice the first thought that pops into your mind. If the answer is no, you will continue your journey today by visiting one of your relative's most influential past lives, a lifetime that will be for your highest good to know about and understand. If the answer is yes, then in just a moment, your guide will take you and your relative back into the past to the most significant lifetime the two of you shared, or to one that will be most for your highest good.

Take your guide and your relative by the hands now and in a moment, the three of you will begin to float. Know that the farther out you float, the earlier the time will be. Allow your guide to take you and your relative to a very early time in your soul's history, to a time that will be most for your highest good.

The three of you will begin to float now. Ready? Floating out, out, out, over the ray of sunshine, you're floating farther and farther and farther into the past, out, out, out to a very early time that will be most for your highest good. You're floating way, way, way back, to this very early event in your soul's history that will give you the most insight into what you are seeking today and what your relative and your guide believe will be most for your highest good.

On the count of three, you will arrive. Ready? One, floating out, out, out; two, farther and farther, you're almost there; and three, you're there. Be there now, floating over this important event.

Imagine you, your relative, and your guide can float down, down, down, down, down, into these events. Be there now and notice what's happening.

What year is this? Notice the first thought that pops into your mind. Where are you in the world? Again, notice your first thoughts. What's happening? Are you alone or with other people?

Imagine you can fast-forward through these events to a moment when you and your relative are together. Be there now. Notice what's happening.

What kind of relationship did you and your relative have in this early time? How does the relationship reflect what you're doing together in your current lifetime? Take your time to notice all you can about exactly what is going on and what is happening between the two of you.

Pause here.

What lessons are your souls learning about in this very early time? How do those lessons relate to your current life? What agreements did your souls make about being together in the same family? Discover and notice any other important details about the connection between you and your relative. Take your time.

Pause here.

Imagine there is a beautiful healing light coming down from above. This loving light is pouring over this lifetime you shared with your relative. Your guide is sending everyone a loving high frequency. Imagine this loving light is encouraging, supportive, and uplifting. Allow your guide to send this light for as long as you would like, allowing everyone to benefit from this extra love and encouragement. Know that everyone involved is now receiving your intention of unconditional love and healing. Both you and your relative easily receive this loving light and both of you are getting lighter and lighter, brighter and brighter.

Pause here.

Continue to process this information as you, your relative, and your guide lift up, up, up, out of these early events, floating higher and higher and higher into the clouds. Send a loving healing light to all people and events from that early time. When you're ready, imagine you and your relative and guide can float back toward today, and as you do, send healing to all your ancestors who lived between those early times and today. The healing light pours into your ray of sunshine, and that light now shines brighter and brighter and lighter and lighter than ever before. Float toward today now. Continue floating toward today, allowing all events between this very early time and today to totally realign in light of this new knowledge and understanding.

In a moment, when you count back from three, you will once again be floating over today. Ready? Three, two, and one; you're back. Still holding your relative and guide by the hand, imagine the three of you can float down, down, down, back through the clouds until you land inside your beautiful room. Be there now, inside your beautiful sacred space. Take a moment to speak with your relative and your guide about anything else of importance. Take your time.

Pause here.

Thank your relative for joining you today. Feel the unconditional love they have for you at a soul level. Take a moment to talk about anything else of importance.

Pause here.

When you're ready, say goodbye; your relative will walk or float back through the door they first came through.

Take a moment to ask your guide for any further clarity you need about this healing.

Pause here.

When you're finished, thank your loving guide for being here today. Say goodbye for now.

Filled with peaceful light, feeling better than you did before, turn around now and walk back through the door you came through. Close the door behind you and go back out to where you began your journey. Be there now, back where you began.

In a moment, when you count from five, you will come back into the room, feeling awake, refreshed, and better than you felt before.

Five—grounded, centered, and balanced. Four—continuing to process this new energy in your dreams tonight so by tomorrow morning, you will be fully integrated into these new insights. Three—still surrounded by that beautiful golden ball of light, safe and protected, you know that only that which is of your highest good can come through. You will drive carefully and be safe in all activities. Two—you're grounded, centered, and balanced, and one—you're back.

•• • ••
JOURNAL PROMPT
Past-Life Regression to
Discover Your Ties to a Living Relative

Take notes about important information you received today. You may want to write down the following.

1. Which living relative or person did you meet today?

2. Did the two of you know each other in past lives?

3. Where did you travel?

4. What year?

5. How will this insight help you understand how your souls agreed to return into the same family or into a common situation such as work during your current incarnation?

There are no accidents in this universe. We choose our families, friends, and situations for our soul growth. Knowing the connections between even your most distant relatives and other prominent people in your life can bring incredible insights into your soul understanding.

Summing Up

The connection you share with your family, friends, and others is meant to be. These relationships are part of your soul contracts that you entered over the course of time. Those people come into your life to help you achieve your purpose, learn lessons, and evolve. You also choose your lineage for your highest learning. There are no accidents. When you deepen the understanding of the people who call you friend or family, even if you're not related by blood, you ultimately come to understand your soul path better than ever before.

Forgiveness and healing are often a lifelong endeavor. You may find patterns from the past still lingering in the present. Awareness and grace are some of the biggest gifts you can give yourself on your journey through Ancestral Energy Healing. I applaud you for your amazing work. You're doing the world a great service through these explorations.

CHAPTER SIX

Rewriting Your History
for Future Generational Healing

Wouldn't it be wonderful to simply rewrite your history and make things more ideal? That's exactly what you can do in this chapter. Through my many years of working in the wacky field of past lives and metaphysics, I've delved into the quantum field extensively to write about parallel worlds and how our inner spiritual work can affect the outer world and future possibilities. Individuals can travel out into their current-life futures, for example, to experience themselves happy, healthy, and fulfilling their purpose. This kind of journey is very powerful. Other times, people go into the past during past-life or Genealogical Regressions to send light to events, and by so doing, they potentially change that past, which ultimately leads to a brighter future. The goal of both processes is to help the client feel better in the now.

Still, this kind of thinking begs the questions I am asked from time to time: Is it okay to change the past? What happens when we do that? Aren't we messing up time by doing so? Those questions bring up an incredibly fascinating concept that's fun to consider called the *Grand-father Paradox*, which has been making an appearance in science fiction stories since at least the 1920s. It goes like this: What would happen if you traveled into the past and accidentally killed your grandfather before he had any children? Surely that would mean you would cease to exist. Then again, if you did do such a thing, then how could you do that if you never existed? This seems like an impossible scenario. For decades, nobody could prove or disprove this idea, so the idea of time traveling became a fun fictional possibility for storytellers.

Thanks to more recent understanding about our world, the Grandfather Paradox has now been solved, according to some scientists. Because of our new comprehension of wormholes and quantum physics, traveling back in time without making any damaging alterations to the present reality may be possible.[14] The study cites the difference between changing our past and simply influencing things. The Ancestral Energy Healing and regression processes involving sending light to forebears and former incarnations might be viewed as mere influence rather than changing things completely. Obviously we can't go back and decide to erase World War II, for example, but we could send light and love to those involved.

Through my many years in practice, I periodically hear from readers who engage me in conversations about such topics that are marginally related to the ideas I write about in my books, which are intended to help people break free from the challenging stories that inform their daily lives and rewrite their reality to one that is more empowering and inspiring.

That's exactly what happens during a past-life regression. People travel into their past lives to an origin point where a current-life problem began. They notice what happened, how they are negatively affected by it, and then make a new decision by either releasing unwanted energies or, in some cases, by totally reinventing the story there. For example, let's say you have a regression and are guided to return to the Middle Ages where you meet with people and observe situations that happened in your prior lifetime. Once that origin point is observed, you can then discuss things with the people involved, and you may choose to make new agreements and then return home to the present day, feel-

---

14. Smith, "Time Travel."

ing refreshed and totally healed and rid of whatever bothered you. If agreements alone don't work, you could go into a scenario where you can totally rewrite the situation to better serve your ideal outcome and soul's purpose.

Reimagining Your Ancestral History

Now that you've experienced Genealogical Regression firsthand, you've discovered that the process is similar to past-life regression, only instead of observing things that your own soul did in prior incarnations, you were able to view and observe events that happened to your ancestors.

You noticed the blessings your ancestors gave you, along with the gifts, talents, and worthy ideals that built your family legacy. Finding the positives in these journeys is a great thing to do because there is so much good to take from the past, whether that's your ancestral past or your past lives.

You also traveled into spaces that were painful, challenging, and unbelievably difficult for your ancestors to endure. What if some of those heavier energies could be relieved by rewriting them? A good example is this: let's say you had an ancestor who behaved badly toward others. It's interesting in this ancestral work to address all people you meet at the soul essence level because then you can have a certain degree of empathy for them. Did they do good by others? No, but coming to this work by asking questions can help us uncover the causes for such horrible behavior. What if some tragedy happened to them earlier in their lives that caused them to behave in a less-than-ideal way to other people they met in their later life? What if those earlier events could be healed for them so that the future for your ancestors could become brighter?

Most of the changes you might make in this regard are emotional rather than changes in history or actual events. For example, if you go into a space where you see an ancestor treating someone badly, you may rewind through their life to go back to places where they were hurt themselves and send them healing and light. If more healing is needed than that, you could totally reimagine the painful interaction they had with the other person by taking it away completely and therefore removing the hurt that affected the entire family line. Once such a healing has been received, that new attitude goes forth from the ancestor receiving the healing and travels through time to make a more positive impact on all people in your lineage who come after them. It's a powerful process. I can't say for sure what will emerge for you, but it can really lighten the heavy load of trauma carried within a family line.

For this exercise, you can either think back to a journey you took from the Genealogical Regression chapter where you encountered an ancestor facing extreme challenge and difficulty and go back into that space, or you may notice a totally new place with a different ancestor who would benefit from this kind of healing. The first part of the journey will be the same as the other, only now we will build into a reimagining of your ancestral history. Recording this in advance is recommended.

•• ● ••
EXERCISE
Reimagining Your Ancestral History

Sit in a comfortable chair with your hands in your lap and feet flat on the floor. Close your eyes. Breathe. Take a deep, healing breath in through your nose, breathing in love and peace and light. Exhale tensions and concerns.

Imagine a beautiful beam of pure white light coming down through the top of your head. Feel that light moving down through your head and forehead, your eyes, your nose, your mouth, and your jaw, moving down, down, down, into your neck and shoulders, into your arms, your elbows, your wrists, your hands and fingertips.

Feel the light moving down, down, down through your shoulders, moving into your heart center. Feel your heart's energy expand as the light continues to move down into your stomach, through your torso to the base of your spine, and into your legs and all the way down into the soles of your feet. Imagine the light flowing quickly from head to feet, and the loving light begins to pour out of your heart center, creating a beautiful golden ball of light that surrounds you by about three feet in all directions. Feel yourself floating inside this peaceful golden ball of light, safe and secure, knowing only that which is of your highest good can come through.

Imagine there's a doorway in front of you. You can see the door, feel the door, or just have an inner knowing the door is there. When you count back from three, you will walk through that door and go inside a beautiful room, into your sacred space. Ready? Three, two, one; you're opening the door. Open the door now and walk or float inside your beautiful room. Be there now.

Take a moment to absorb the wonderful feelings of peace and harmony. Allow this place to fill your body with loving light and healing energy.

Pause here.

As you continue to enjoy your sacred space, your loving guide floats down to join you. Imagine they are with you right now. Feel the unconditional love they have for you.

Take a moment to discuss your intentions for today. Let your guide know you would like to meet with one of your parents to heal and reimagine a challenging event that affected your family. If you know which parent and which ancestral line you want to explore, let them know that also. Take your time to discuss all you need.

Pause here.

Once you finish speaking with your guide, notice there's a door on the other side of your room. That door is opening now, and here comes one of your parents. Remember this is their Higher Self, the soul essence of your parent. Notice them now. Who is this? Notice the first thought that comes into your mind. Feel the essence of their soul and notice how happy your parent is to see you.

Imagine you can let your parent know that you would like to reimagine a challenging event that affected the family. Know that your parent and guide can assist you in knowing which event is best. Let them both know that you want to visit the event that is most in need of healing at this moment, the event that would make the most positive impact on your entire lineage. Receive clarity about which side of your parent's family you are going to visit today.

Pause here.

When you're ready, imagine you and your parent can take your guide by the hand, and the three of you begin to float toward that door your parent came through. In just a moment, when you count to three, the door will open and you and your guide and your parent will float through that door, and you will find yourselves traveling in the clouds, floating out over a ray of sunshine that represents your ancestral history. On the count of one, you will open that door. Ready? Three, two, and one; you're opening that door now.

Float through the door and be there now, floating in the clouds over a ray of sunshine. Know that this healing sunbeam represents time and your ancestral history. Imagine you are floating over today, and the ray of sunshine stretches on for as far as your eye can see. Know that the farther out you float, the earlier the time will be. Allow your guide to take you and your parent to a very early time in your ancestral history, the time that will be for your highest good.

Know that today, you, your parent, and your guide are going back in time to a moment in your ancestor's past to identify and heal a challenging situation that affected your entire lineage. The three of you will begin now to float. Ready? Floating out, out, out, over the ray of sunshine, you're floating out, out, out to a very early time that will be most for your highest good. Know that the farther out you float, the earlier the time will be.

You're floating way, way, way back, to this very early event in your lineage that will give you the most insights into what you are seeking today and what your parent and your guide believe will be most for your and your family's highest good.

On the count of three, you will arrive. Ready? One, floating out, out, out; two, farther and farther, you're almost there; and three, you're there. Be there now, floating over this important time in your ancestral history.

Imagine you and your parent and your guide can float down, down, down, down, down, and hover over these events. Remember you are still surrounded by a protective shield of golden light. Within the light, you are safe and protected and able to view these events easily. Be there now and notice what's happening.

What year is this? Notice the first thought that pops into your mind. Where are you in the world? Again, notice your first thoughts. What's happening? Which ancestor or ancestors do you see? Imagine you can easily sense or feel the energy of your ancestors.

Take your time to notice all you can about exactly what is going on and what is happening to your ancestor. If needed, imagine you can fast-forward through these events to the situation most in need of healing today.

Pause here.

Imagine there is a beautiful healing light coming down from above. This loving light is pouring over this event and sending a loving high frequency to your ancestors and all who are involved in this event. Imagine this energy is getting lighter and lighter and lighter, brighter and brighter and brighter. Allow your loving light to raise the vibrations and frequencies around these challenging events. Imagine you, your parent, and your guide can easily send this light for as long as you would like.

Pause here.

As you continue to send the loving light, you notice the heavy energy surrounding these events begins to feel more peaceful than before. As you notice the light, imagine you can understand how your ancestor felt and what brought them to the events they are now enduring. Take a moment and rewind to a much earlier time in their life that may better explain how they experience their life. Imagine you can return to an early event in their life that needs healing. Be there now; notice what's happening.

Pause here.

What year are you visiting? What is happening to your ancestor? How did this situation impact them as they grew up?

Pause here.

If possible, take a moment to reimagine how this event could have been more peaceful. Take your time and allow your guide and parent to assist you in reimagining the early event that happened to your ancestor. Take your time to notice a new reality.

Pause here.

Very good. Imagine that you can easily see how this new event is lighter and far brighter than the original event. Notice now how much better your ancestor feels in this new reality. Take your time and imagine you can move forward in time through your ancestor's life with this new energy and based on this new lighter reality. Notice key moments where your ancestor feels far better and enjoys an easier life because of this new reality.

Pause here.

When you're ready, go back to the event you originally visited during this journey. Notice now how much differently your ancestor reacts thanks to the lighter earlier influences they experienced. Notice how much kinder and calmer they are or any other positive differences this shift has made in their life. Imagine you can notice how this positive influence ripples through time and imagine it can positively affect every single person in your family line. As this happens, know that a beautiful loving light is coming down and healing everyone you've encountered today, including your ancestor.

Pause here.

Know that you are making an impact by sending this loving healing light. Know that the light you, your parent, and your guide are sending is making an incredible impact on everyone. As you notice that energy, you can also see that there is an energetic cord of light connecting you and your parent to this very early event. These light cords are coming out of your stomach or solar plexus areas and connecting you with these ancestors and the events below you.

Your guide is now holding a big pair of golden scissors. In a moment, when you count from three, your guide will cut the cords between you and your parent and these very early ancestors and events. Ready? Three, two, one; your guide is cutting the cords now.

As these cords are cut, the light pouring down from above now moves through you and your parent, and both of you are getting lighter and lighter and lighter and brighter and brighter and brighter. That healing light extends now to all the family members in your lineage as your entire family becomes lighter and brighter, lighter than ever before.

Take a moment while this healing energy refreshes you and notice how much better you feel. Notice how much lighter and brighter your parent looks and feels.

As you continue to receive this healing, imagine you and your parent can ask your loving guide to explain the lessons you and your family learned from this experience. Take your time and receive all the details you need as you continue to receive this healing light.

Pause here.

Continue to process this information as you, your parent, and your guide continue to send healing light to this very early time in your ancestral history.

Imagine you and your parent and your guide can lift up, up, up, out of these early events, floating higher and higher and higher into the clouds. Hold hands with your parent and guide and the three of you will begin now to float back toward today, but only as quickly as you can notice how this new reality has positively impacted everyone in your family tree. Moving forward toward today, you and your parent and guide continue to send that loving healing light to all events and all ancestors between these early times and today. Imagine this healing light pours into your ray of sunshine, making that light shine brighter and brighter and lighter and lighter than ever before. Float toward today now. Floating farther and farther, forward in time, allowing all events to heal and transform. Continue floating toward today, allowing all events between that very early event and today to totally realign in light of this new understanding and healing.

When you count back from three, you will be back, floating over today. Ready? Three, two, and one; you're back. Float back through the door you came through. Close that door behind you and go back into your beautiful room and sacred space. Be there now, back inside your sacred space.

Take a moment to speak with your parent and your guide about anything else of importance. Discuss any big changes that happened once you reimagined the past. Take your time.

Pause here.

Thank your parent for joining you today. Once again, feel the unconditional love they have for you at a soul level. Take a moment to talk about anything else of importance.

Pause here.

When you're ready, say goodbye and imagine your parent will walk or float back through the door they first came through earlier.

Take a moment to ask your guide for any further clarity you need about this healing.

Pause here.

When you're finished, thank your loving guide for being here today. Say goodbye for now and watch your guide float back to where they came from. Know that you will see your guide again soon.

Take a deep breath in through your nose and allow yourself to become completely relaxed inside your sacred space. Allow the supportive energies of your sacred space to move through every single cell of your being. As you do, breathe in the energy of joy, peace, and happiness as you inhale one, two, three, four, and exhale love and light, one, two, three, four. Very good.

Filled with peaceful light, feeling better than you did before, turn around now and walk back through the door you came through. Close the door behind you and go back out to where you began your journey. Be there now, back where you began.

In a moment, when you count from five, you will come back into the room, feeling awake, refreshed, and better than you felt before.

Five—grounded, centered, and balanced. Four—continuing to process this new energy in your dreams tonight so by tomorrow morning, you will be fully integrated into these new insights. Three—still surrounded by that beautiful golden ball of light, safe and protected, you know that only that which is of your highest good can come through. You will drive carefully and be safe in all activities. Two—you're grounded, centered, and balanced, and one—you're back.

•• ● ••
JOURNAL PROMPT
Reimagining Your Ancestral History

Take your time to write down what happened and keep track of important changes.

1. Which parent did you meet?
2. What scenario did you see at first and why was it so challenging to your ancestor?
3. What happened in your ancestor's early past that affected their outlook on life?
4. How did you reimagine their early life?
5. What impact did that new lighter reality have on your ancestor?
6. How did their behavior change?
7. How does this new reality positively affect everyone in your lineage?

Be sure to keep track of any dreams, residual thoughts, or insights you have about this healing.

Rewriting Your Ancestral History

One way to go even deeper with this kind of healing is to go back through the notes you've made on prior Genealogical Regressions and use your journal to write more about the events and rewrite them in your Ancestral Healing journal. Bringing the ideas of your mind, heart, and soul into the physical by writing them down will help firmly shift things in three-dimensional reality. The following exercise is one you will do in writing. I encourage you to repeat these steps as needed when you're guided to do so.

•• ● ••

EXERCISE AND JOURNAL PROMPT
Rewriting Your Ancestral History

In this exercise, sit in your comfortable space and take some time when you won't be disturbed to get your journal out and take some notes. Here are the steps:

1. Think of an event from your family history.
   - Stories told to you by your parents or other family members
   - Things you've uncovered on ancestral research sites
   - Scenarios uncovered during Genealogical Regression
   - Events discovered from the Reimagining Your Ancestral History exercise
   - Any other event (obviously, there are a lot of possibilities to choose from, so pick one you believe is for your highest good at this moment)

2. Pull out your journal and write the event down as you recall hearing it or how you perceived it as you learned the details.

3. Once you've documented things as they are according to your understanding, take some time and open your mind to ways

this event could have been more advantageous and less traumatic for your ancestors. This may involve the following:

- Imagining what would happen if certain people didn't die
- Projecting what could occur if illness or other calamity had been avoided

    Remember, there's literally no end to the possibilities of what you could rewrite here. For now, just put your mind into free flow mode and write down any thoughts, feelings, and ideas.

4. Next, once you get all your free-flowing ideas down in writing, notice which possibility feels best to you.

5. Once you've selected your favorite, write down the new reality in detail.

6. As you write, notice how this new reality affects your ancestor and their family and people they knew during their lifetime.

7. Project this new positive outcome into your ancestor's future. Imagine how this new way of being might make an incredibly positive impact on the descendants of your ancestor. Write it all down.

8. Next, imagine your parent becoming healed and relieved in light of this new reality.

9. Notice how you feel after recreating your ancestral past. Feel the improved vitality within and write down how that feels.

10. How might this new energy benefit you in the future?

11. What do you think future generations of your family may experience as a result of this new family history?

12. How has your family's future improved over what may have happened had they not received this light, healing, and attention?

13. How did this exercise make you feel?

14. Could you sense energetic improvements by rewriting the history of your lineage?

Keep making notes of any subtle changes or insights you may receive later. Remember to take your time and write down anything you think works best for you above and beyond my suggestions. The idea here is to play with your positive creativity a bit and write the story that will give you and your family the best outcome. Doing so can yield positive outcomes and new insights down the road.

Reimagining Your Past Lives

The idea of having a do-over for your family is incredibly empowering, and although the DNA brings our ancestors into our energy more than anything else I can think of, your past lives also influence your current life tremendously in ways you may not be consciously aware of all the time. You experienced that firsthand in the section on past-life regression.

What if you could also go back through and reimagine those former incarnations to better empower and serve you in the here and now? That's what you will do right now. Since you're working on Ancestral Healing, this journey will focus on healing a past life that you potentially uncovered earlier between you and a parental figure or you and an ancestor or family member. You may work on something that occurred to you during your past-life regression journeys, or something totally new may come up. Also remember that the person who shows up could be a grandparent, aunt, uncle, foster parent, or even a friend or coworker. Regardless of who appears, the healing potential can be amazing and will be for your highest good. For the journey, I will again refer to this special someone as your relative.

•• ● ••
EXERCISE
Reimagining Your Past Lives

Retreat to your personal sacred space and relax. Close your eyes. Imagine feeling a beautiful beam of light coming down from above and moving through every cell of your body and flowing around you in a golden swirl of protective energy. Notice the doorway that leads to your sacred space. Open the door and walk or float into your beautiful room. Be there now.

Your guide is there waiting for you. Say hello. Take a moment now to discuss your intentions for today. Let your guide know that you would like to meet with one of your parents, family members, or ancestors to heal and reimagine a challenging past-life event that affected you both. If you know which relative you want to explore, let them know that also. Take your time to discuss all you need.

Pause here.

Once you finish speaking with your guide, notice there's a door on the other side of your room. That door is opening now, and here comes one of your relatives or another significant person in your life. Remember this is their Higher Self, the soul essence. Notice them now. Who is this? Notice the first thought that comes into your mind. Feel the essence of their soul and notice how happy they are to see you.

Imagine you can let them know that you would like to reimagine a challenging event that affected you in your past lives. Know that your relative and guide can assist you in knowing which event is best. Let them both know that you want to visit the event that is most in need of healing at this moment, the event that would make the most positive impact on your entire lineage. Receive clarity about the event you are going to visit today.

Pause here.

When you're ready, imagine you and your relative can take your guide by the hand and the three of you begin to float toward that door your relative came through. In just a moment, when you count to three, the door will open and you and your guide and your relative will float through that door, and you will find yourselves traveling in the clouds, floating out over a ray of sunshine that represents your shared past lives. On the count of one, you will open that door. Ready? Three, two, and one; you're opening that door now.

Float through the door and be there now, floating in the clouds over a ray of sunshine. Know that this healing sunbeam represents time and your shared past lives. Imagine you are floating over today, and the ray of sunshine stretches on for as far as your eye can see. Know that the farther out you float, the earlier the time will be. Allow your guide to take you and your relative to a very early time in your soul's history, the time that will be for your highest good at this moment.

Know that today, you, your relative, and your guide are going back in time to a moment in your past to identify and heal a challenging situation that may affect your entire lineage. The three of you will begin now to float. Ready? Floating out, out, out, over the ray of sunshine, you're floating to a very early time that will be most for your highest good. Know that the farther out you float, the earlier the time will be.

You're floating way, way, way back, to this very early event in your shared past lives that will give you the most insights into what you are seeking today and what your relative and your guide believe will be most for your and everyone's highest good.

On the count of three, you will arrive. Ready? One, floating out, out, out; two, farther and farther, you're almost there; and three, you're there. Be there now, floating over this important time.

Imagine you and your relative and your guide can float down, down, down, down, down, and hover over these events. Remember you are still surrounded by a protective shield of golden light. Within the light, you are safe and protected and able to view these events easily. Be there now and notice what's happening.

What year is this? Notice the first thought that pops into your mind. Where are you in the world? Again, notice your first thoughts. What's happening? Which relative or relatives do you see? Imagine you can easily sense or feel their energy.

Take your time to notice all you can about exactly what is going on and what is happening between you and your relative. If needed, imagine you can fast-forward through these events to the situation most in need of healing today.

Pause here.

Imagine there is a beautiful healing light coming down from above. This loving light is pouring over this event and sending a loving high frequency to you, your relative, and all who are involved in this event. Imagine this energy is getting lighter and lighter and lighter, brighter and brighter and brighter. Allow your loving light to raise the vibrations and frequencies around these challenging events. Imagine you, your relative, and your guide can easily send this light for as long as you would like.

Pause here.

As you continue to send the loving light, you notice the heavy energy surrounding these events begins to feel more peaceful than before. As you notice the light, imagine you can understand how your ancestor felt and what brought them to the events they are now enduring. Take a moment and rewind to a much earlier time in their life or even their childhood that may better explain how they experience their life. Imagine you can return to an early event in their life that needs healing. Be there now; notice what's happening.

Pause here.

What year are you visiting? What is happening? How does this situation impact you in your current lifetime?

Pause here.

If possible, take a moment to reimagine how this event could have been more peaceful. Take your time and allow your guide and relative to assist you in reimagining this early event. Take your time to notice a new reality now.

Pause here.

Very good. Imagine that you can easily see how this new event is lighter and far brighter than the original event. Notice now how much better you, your relative, and all others feel in this new reality. Take your time and imagine you can move forward through your ancestor's life with this new energy and based on this new lighter reality. Notice key moments where your ancestor feels far better and enjoys an easier life as a result of this new reality.

Pause here.

When you're ready, go back to the event you originally visited during this journey. Notice now how much differently your relative reacts thanks to the healing you've done today. Notice positive differences this shift has made. Notice how this positive influence ripples through time and imagine it can positively affect every single person in your family line. As this happens, know that a beautiful loving light is coming down and healing everyone you've encountered today, including your relative.

Pause here.

Know that you are making an impact by sending this loving healing light. Know that the light you, your relative, and your guide are sending is making an incredible impact on everyone. As you notice that energy, you can also see that there is an energetic cord of light connecting you and your relative to this very early event. These light cords are coming out of your stomach or solar plexus areas and connecting you with this relative and the events below you.

Your guide is now holding a big pair of golden scissors. When you count from three, your guide will cut the cords between you and your relative and these very early events. Ready? Three, two, one; your guide is cutting the cords now.

As these cords are cut, you notice the light pouring down from above now moves through you and your relative and both of you are getting lighter and lighter and lighter and brighter and brighter and brighter. That healing light extends now to all the family members in your lineage as your entire family becomes lighter and brighter, lighter than ever before.

Take a moment while this healing energy refreshes you and notice how much better you feel. Notice how much lighter and brighter your relative looks and feels.

As you continue to receive this healing, imagine you and your relative can ask your loving guide to explain the lessons you learned from this experience. Take your time and receive all the details you need as you continue to receive this healing light.

Pause here.

Continue to process this information as you, your relative, and your guide continue to send healing light to this very early time in your soul's history.

Imagine you and your relative and your guide can lift up, up, up, out of these early events, floating higher and higher and higher into the clouds. Hold hands with your relative and guide and the three of you will begin now to float back toward today, but only as quickly as you can notice how this new reality has positively impacted everyone in your family tree. Moving forward toward today, you and your relative and guide continue to send that loving healing light to all events between these early times and today. Imagine this healing light pours into your ray of sunshine, making that light shine brighter and brighter and lighter and lighter than ever before. Float toward today now. Floating farther and farther, forward in time, allowing all events to heal and transform now. Continue floating toward today, allowing all events between that very early event and today to totally realign in light of this new understanding and healing.

When you count back from three, you will be back, floating over today. Ready? Three, two, and one; you're back. Float back through the door you came through. Close that door behind you and go back into your beautiful room and sacred space. Be there now, back inside your sacred space.

Take a moment to speak with your relative and guide about anything else of importance. Discuss any big changes that happened once you reimagined the past. Take your time.

Pause here.

Thank your relative for joining you today. Once again feel the unconditional love they have for you at a soul level. Take a moment to talk about anything else of importance.

Pause here.

When you're ready, say goodbye and imagine your relative will walk or float back through the door they first came through.

Take a moment to ask your guide for any further clarity you need about this healing.

Pause here.

When you're finished, thank your loving guide for being here today. Say goodbye for now.

Filled with peaceful light, feeling better than you did before, turn around now and walk back through the door. Close the door behind you and go back out to where you began your journey. Be there now, back where you began.

In a moment, when you count from five, you will come back into the room, feeling awake, refreshed, and better than you felt before.

Five—grounded, centered, and balanced. Four—continuing to process this new energy in your dreams tonight so by tomorrow morning, you will be fully integrated into these new insights. Three—still surrounded by that beautiful golden ball of light, safe and protected, you know that only that which is of your highest good can come through. You will drive carefully and be safe in all activities. Two—you're grounded, centered, and balanced, and one—you're back.

•• ● ••
JOURNAL PROMPT
Reimagining Your Past Lives

Take your time to write down what happened and keep track of important changes.

1. Which relative did you meet with today?
2. What past life did you visit?
3. What happened and how did you reimagine the events?

This is definitely an exercise that could be experienced more than once because we have so many past-life connections with many of our family members and relatives.

Rewriting Your Past Lives

Now that you've opened your imagination to perceiving a better outcome for past lives you shared with your relative, you can do what you did earlier and commit those positive changes to paper.

•• ● ••
EXERCISE AND JOURNAL PROMPT
Rewriting Your Past Lives

Pull out your journal and consider the following.

1. What past life did you explore in the last exercise?
2. Take your time and rewrite events for a positive outcome.
3. Consider what emerged when you reimagined these events, and if needed, make your new story even better.
4. After completing the earlier steps, make more notes about any other thoughts you have about doing that process.
5. Wait awhile and see how you feel over time. Perhaps you notice your feelings in a few days, then wait a week, then check in after a month. Write about any positive changes you experience by rewriting your past lives.

6. What other feelings did you have after rewriting past lives?

7. What positive outcomes could you imagine for your future?

8. Were you able to sense that healing past lives could help your lineage? If so, how?

As usual, keep going with any other important details that can help you later. Since you're busy living your life, this might be something that floats in over time, when you least expect it. You may be doing something in the future and, all of a sudden, you realize you're not triggered by something that used to be bothersome. You may experience increased feelings of peace or ease. Again, there's no one-size-fits-all here. How you receive your newly minted past life is up to you.

Future Generational Healing

Ancestral Healing has many incredible benefits that we can enjoy in our current lifetimes, including healing, forgiving, resolving old conflicts and emotional wounds, and enjoying greater peace, happiness, and overall vitality in our lives by releasing incredibly old energies. Healing ourselves is so powerful in reshaping every single challenge that we face today.

The art of forgiveness is also paramount to helping us become happier and therefore more productive and positive contributors to the world around us.

Still, beyond our own selves, it's clear that Ancestral Healing is something we initially engage in to be of service to others. The others we focus on are those brave and courageous ancestors who carved out a path so that you and I can be here now to carry on this conversation. We want to love and honor them and send them light and hope to relieve some of the tremendous pressure, pain, and often agony that must have occurred in their lifetimes.

By engaging in these selfless acts of kindness for our forebears, we invariably help ourselves with the increased vitality and other benefits just mentioned, but where does this work go beyond that?

When you think about it, healing ourselves must help people in the future who have yet to be born, and I'm not just talking about our family members. Everyone in the entire world is helped tremendously when you and I take a moment, or two or three, to get in touch with our souls and do some much-needed healing, creating more peace within ourselves. When we are grounded and operating from a place of greater love and tolerance toward others, then every single person, plant, animal, or being who encounters us will be engaging with a better version of ourselves. Nobody's perfect. We all know that. Healing is often a lifelong endeavor. Showing up for others and doing so in a more peaceful way today than we felt yesterday means everyone benefits from our new state of calm and well-being.

By now, you've seen how you can travel forward in time and bless everybody who lived in your family lineage between the earliest and most troubled times and today. The good feelings you create by sending love and light can be quite calming. Even if that sensation is subtle, you can often sense how much better your ancestors feel compared to how they felt or appeared before you sent the healing.

That means that as all your lineage moves forward in time, those family members who have yet to be born are going to reap the benefits from the work you're doing. When you heal, you're not the same person who began the healing in the first place. You're filled with more love, grace, and compassion than ever before. Those new higher frequencies become infused into your DNA and that energy is carried forward to future family members who are not even born yet.

In 1955, just weeks before his death, Albert Einstein observed that "the distinction between past, present and future is only a stubbornly persistent illusion."[15] The idea that all time is now has persisted within popular culture and is a mainstay for understanding how and why past-life regression or any other regression method works. When I guided my clients into their current-life futures where their challenges were

---

15. Wolchover, "Does Time Really Flow?"

resolved, that implied that if they followed the steps needed to create that future, they could heal and transform things in the real world.

Likewise, while you and I will not see all these new people who will be here after we're gone and theoretically there's no way to prove these methods work, I feel confident that when you send light to the past, it ripples forward through time and benefits the future, and in this case, your *future ancestors*.

In this next exercise, you will have a chance to send much-needed light to the future generations of your family. Similar to the other journeys, you will need to decide which side of the family you would like to begin with. You can repeat the journey again and again until all the possibilities are covered and you've succeeded in sending light to the future. It's an amazing feeling to do so. I will again be referring to the person as your parent, so keep that in mind while inviting whoever appears to show up for you. Also, this is a great journey to prerecord.

•• ● ••

EXERCISE
Future Generational Healing

Sit in your comfortable chair with your hands in your lap and feet flat on the floor. Close your eyes. Breathe. Take a deep, healing breath in through your nose, breathing in love and peace and light. Exhale tensions and concerns.

Imagine a beam of pure white light moving from head to feet, healing you, relaxing you, and carrying away any stress or tension. Very good.

This loving light is getting stronger now and begins to pour out of your heart center, creating a beautiful golden ball of light that surrounds you by about three feet in all directions. Feel yourself floating inside this peaceful golden ball of light, and know that within this golden light, only that which is of your highest good can come through.

You notice the doorway that leads to your personal sacred space. When you count back from three, you will walk through that door and go inside your beautiful room. Ready? Three, two, one; you're opening the door. Open the door now and walk or float inside your beautiful room. Be there now.

Take a moment to absorb the wonderful feelings of peace and harmony. Your loving guide floats down to join you. Discuss your intentions for today. Let your guide know that you would like to meet with one of your parents to send loving light to future generations of your family. If you know which parent and which ancestral line you want to explore, let your guide know that also. Take your time to discuss all you need.

Pause here.

Once you finish speaking with your guide, notice there's a door on the other side of your room. That door is opening now, and here comes one of your parents. Remember this is their Higher Self, the soul essence of your parent. Notice them now. Who is this? Notice the first thought that comes into your mind. Feel the essence of their soul and notice how happy your parent is to see you.

Imagine you can let your parent know that you would like to visit a future generation of your family to send them light. Take your time to explain this to your parent and imagine that they and your guide can assist you in knowing which lineage you will visit first. Take a moment to receive clarity about which side of your parent's family you are going to visit today.

Pause here.

When you're ready, imagine you and your parent can take your guide by the hand and the three of you begin now to float. You're floating up, up, up, out of the beautiful room where you started, up, up, up, into the clouds, floating so high in the sky, you find yourselves floating out over a ray of sunshine that represents time. Imagine you are floating over today, and the ray of sunshine stretches on for as far as your eye can see. Imagine you can look back toward the past and notice how bright the past seems thanks to the healing you have done so far. Then imagine you can glance out into the direction of your family's future.

Know that today, you, your parent, and your guide are going forward in time to the future to observe and send love and light to a future generation of your family lineage.

The three of you will begin now to float. Ready? Floating out, out, out, over the ray of sunshine, you're floating to a future event that will be most for your highest good. Know that the farther out you float, the later the time will be.

You're floating out, out, out, into this far-reaching event in your family lineage that will be most for your highest good and of the greatest benefit to your entire family.

On the count of three, you will arrive. Ready? One, floating out, out, out; two, farther and farther, you're almost there; and three, you're there. Be there now, floating over this important time in your ancestral future.

Imagine you and your parent and your guide can float down, down, down, down, down, and hover over these events. Be there now and notice what's happening.

What year is this? Notice the first thought that pops into your mind. Where are you in the world? Again, notice your first thoughts. What's happening? Which future family members do you see? Imagine you can easily sense or feel the energy of your future generations. Take your time to notice all you can about exactly what is going on and what is happening to your family.

Pause here.

Imagine there is a beautiful healing light coming down from above. This loving light is pouring over this event and sending a loving high frequency to your family and all who are involved in this event. Imagine this loving light is encouraging, supportive, and uplifting. Send this light for as long as you would like, allowing everyone to benefit from this extra love and encouragement. Know that your family and everyone involved in these events are now receiving your intention of unconditional love and healing.

Imagine that you and your parent can also receive this loving light and both of you are getting lighter and lighter, brighter and brighter.

As you continue to observe these events, what gifts and talents are being revealed? How do these events and happenings relate to your soul's purpose that may or may not be shared with your entire lineage and family? How do these events represent the legacy of your entire family and how the work you've been doing in Ancestral Energy Healing has helped them?

As you all continue to receive this healing, imagine you and your parent can ask your loving guide to explain the lessons you and your family learned from this experience of witnessing the positive effects of your efforts in Ancestral Healing. Take your time and receive all the details you need as you continue to receive this healing light.

Pause here.

Continue to process this information as you, your parent, and your guide continue to send healing light to this moment in your future family history. Allow this healing to continue as you and your parent and your guide lift up, up, up, out of these future events, floating higher and higher and higher into the clouds. As you float over these events, continue to send loving healing light to all your descendants, other people, and events in that future time. When you're ready, imagine you, your parent, and your guide can float back toward the present day, and as you do, you can continue to send love and light to all family members between those future times and today. Imagine this new knowledge assists and inspires everyone in your family tree from the earliest times in your ancestry all the way through to the present day and will continue to benefit those future ancestors who have yet to be born. As the knowledge of your gifts and this healing light pours into your ray of sunshine, that light now shines brighter and brighter and lighter and lighter than ever before. Float toward today now. Continue floating toward today, back in time from the future, allowing all events between this future time in your lineage and today to totally realign in light of this new knowledge and understanding.

In a moment, when you count back from three, you will once again be floating over today. Ready? Three, two, and one; you're back. Still holding hands with your parent and your guide, the three of you will float down, down, down, and back through the clouds and land back inside your beautiful room. Be there now inside your beautiful sacred space. Be there now.

Take a moment to speak with your parent and your guide about anything else of importance. Take your time.

Pause here.

Thank your parent for joining you today. Once again feel the unconditional love they have for you at a soul level. Take a moment to talk about anything else of importance.

Pause here.

When you're ready, say goodbye; your parent will walk or float back through the door they first came through.

Take a moment to ask your guide for any further clarity you need about this healing.

Pause here.

When you're finished, thank your loving guide for being here today. Say goodbye for now and watch your guide float back to where they came from. Know that you will see your guide again soon.

Take a deep breath in through your nose and allow yourself to become completely relaxed inside your sacred space. Allow the supportive energies of your sacred space to move through every single cell of your being. As you do, breathe in the energy of joy, peace, and happiness as you inhale one, two, three, four, and exhale love and light, one, two, three, four. Very good.

Filled with peaceful light, feeling better than you did before, turn around now and walk back through the door you came through. Close the door behind you and go back out to where you began your journey. Be there now, back where you began.

In a moment, when you count from five, you will come back into the room, feeling awake, refreshed, and better than you felt before.

Five—grounded, centered, and balanced. Four—continuing to process this new energy in your dreams tonight so by tomorrow morning, you will be fully integrated into these new insights. Three—still surrounded by that beautiful golden ball of light, safe and protected, you know that only that which is of your highest good can come through. You will drive carefully and be safe in all activities. Two—you're grounded, centered, and balanced, and one—you're back.

Keep in mind that you could repeat this for each side of your family or for adoptive, foster, or other caregivers.

•• ● ••

JOURNAL PROMPT
Future Generational Healing

Take some time to make note of all the valuable information you received today. Here are a few suggestions for things you may want to write down.

1. Which parental figure met you today?
2. Which side of the family did you and your parental figure explore?
3. Where did you travel in the future?
4. What year did you visit?
5. What experiences and activities did your future family members engage in?
6. Did you sense that they had a better life thanks to your Ancestral Energy Healing work?
7. Did you sense that the healing light, love, and encouragement you shared with them helped them even more than before you arrived?

8. How do your current-life actions benefit the future members of your family?

9. Did you sense that helping future generations is part of your life's purpose, and if so, how can that understanding help you in the future?

Keep these thoughts and feelings in mind and continue to note any other insights you find helpful.

Summing Up

Reimagining your ancestor's experiences and wishing things could have been more peaceful for them is a loving and kind thing to do. Energizing that feeling through writing the ideal history you wish to experience can help relieve the heavier emotional scars left by wars, pandemics, and the perils of daily living and therefore leave less heaviness in the energetic field surrounding your lineage.

Emotions are what will likely shift the most when you do this kind of healing. When your emotions are calmer and more loving, that love and light extend farther to everyone you meet both now and into your own future, as well as into the future of those yet to be born. If Einstein really was correct and all time is an illusion, when you send this new vision for a brighter past into your ancestral history, your present and future shift and evolve to a higher state of being, creating greater joy, peace, and love for all concerned.

Feeling the loving energies and pull of those who have yet to be born may surely help you connect to the deeper meaning and purpose behind the wonderful work you're doing on behalf of your family or other caregivers and parental figures. When you sense a change for the better in your own life, that's one thing, but knowing that future people are going to live better lives thanks to your time and effort will hopefully bring you a feeling of great joy and a wider sense of your soul's purpose.

Part Three

Ancestral Energy Healing

In this section, I will share some incredible yet simple exercises you can do to acknowledge your ancestors within your own body. By bringing conscious awareness to places within yourself where ancestral energy resides, you can be more attuned to what areas need your love and attention to shift, heal, and transform. We will explore the term *embodied* and what it truly means to be present in your body to experience all life has to offer. Over the past few years, I've come to understand just how important embodiment is if we want to heal ourselves and our ancestors.

The effort is well worth it. The practices you will explore here are simple yet profound. I've been doing these for years now and shared the methods with students and clients who received incredible results by doing them. I hope these exercises can bring you positive shifts in your awareness and help you on your path to healing on behalf of your lineage.

CHAPTER SEVEN
. . . .
Embodied Exercises
for Ancestral Energy Healing

The term *embodied* seems to be thrown around a lot these days, especially by healers and lightworkers. Have you ever stopped to consider what that term even means? *Embodied* implies something quite profound—*in body*—meaning that you must actually be in your body in order to do these practices and methods. What a concept!

Back when I first began doing hypnosis, guided imagery, and past-life regressions, we did not have all the content and electronics we do now. People were truly bogged down in their daily lives and experienced heavy energy. I did a ton of energy healing during those days. I remember instructing my healing students that helping clients escape the troubling lower-vibrational frequencies around this planet, if only for an hour, should be their ultimate goal. Helping people get up and leave the body energetically, float out into a wider and more expansive place, gain wisdom or peace, and return would bring clients that greater cosmic awareness and inner calm they could carry with them into their daily lives.

What a difference a couple decades can make! Our world has certainly changed. These days, thanks to our technological breakthroughs, all people are engaged in escapism of some kind from the moment they get up in the morning to the moment they lay their heads down on the pillow at night.

The invention of the iPhone, brought to us by the late great visionary Steve Jobs, caused this profound shift in planetary consciousness. Now, we can read, listen to music or podcasts, surf the internet, chat it up with our friends, or escape reality altogether with fictional stories through other content. The weird thing is that we used to have conversations with each other, but now, everybody is totally engaged in a world of their own creation. People explore their own interests on an individual level through various content platforms rather than conversing with each other in the outer world. Earlier we discussed the outer and inner worlds. These days, everybody spends a high percentage of their daily lives within their own inner worlds. It's quite a shift, to say the least.

While we can all be thankful for certain advances that dramatically assisted humankind, I have long been hugely opposed to technology and social media in general. Although I am grateful for the ability to get my own material out to the world thanks to certain revolutionary breakthroughs in publishing, I am simultaneously disturbed more than ever by the destruction tech has on people, especially the younger generation. You would think that having everything handed to us and available at our fingertips 24-7 would make everybody happy. In recent years, we've learned that's not true. Studies find more than ever these days that individuals are unhappy, and often suicidal, faced with epic levels of despair and depression. Global suicide rates exploded to a staggering 800,000 per year, and suicide is now the second leading cause of death for our youth.[16] This is a horrific situation we must address and face as a society. Our disconnected tech environment is largely to blame.

What's missing in our lives, you ask? What could make the difference between hope and despair? *Grounding.* Connecting to earth is fun-

---

16. Martinez-Ales et al., "Why Are Suicide Rates Increasing in the United States?" 1–23.

damental to our well-being. We must make a conscious effort to be grounded. To do that, we must get off our devices, despite how addictive they can be. We can also learn exercises to help.

The work in this chapter is about grounding. It's about finding your way back from wherever it is you've gone off to so you can get back into your own body, feel the feelings and emotions of daily life, and by so doing, experience the release of the stuck energies that are within all of us. That's the path to happiness—*being here*. I've come back to life myself, and I can assure you, doing so can change your circumstances for the better. Likewise, as so many these days are called to the arduous task of healing the ancestors, to do that, we must reconnect with the earth where our ancestors once struggled, thrived, and lived. What I like most about the ideas I will share with you in this chapter is the fact that you can use these processes to do Ancestral Energy Healing without getting into the challenging emotions and feelings that may come up in other exercises described in the book. Using your own personal energy, movement, and strength, you can achieve tremendous benefits on your path of Ancestral Energy Healing.

Planes of Motion

To become a more grounded, embodied person, you can learn simple movement exercises. Before we get into those, we must discuss the planes of motion. Within your body, there are three directions your body can move and flow in:

- **Frontal Plane**—Divides the front of your body from the back.
- **Transverse Plane**—Divides your body in two at the waist.
- **Sagittal Plane**—Divides the body by the left and right sides.

We will explore each of these through some simple movement exercises, and I'll show you how they relate to your Ancestral Healing and finding the ancestors within you.

Movement within the Frontal Plane

The Frontal Plane divides your body from front to back. You can imagine an invisible line moving through the top of your head, traveling down through the body, and dividing the front of your chest from your back, your kneecaps from the backs of your knees and legs, and so forth.

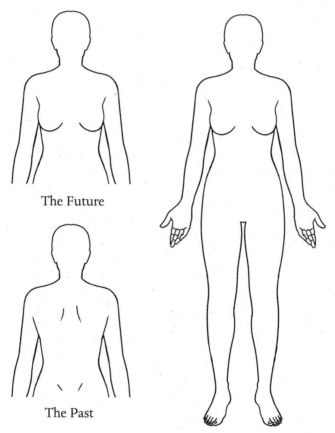

Image 1: Frontal Plane

Spiritually speaking, the front of your body represents the future. The energy on your back represents the past. You will utilize that concept further in the next chapter on Ancestral Energy Healing.

•• ● ••
EXERCISE
Movement within the Frontal Plane

For now, let's do a quick exercise to bring more awareness into this part of your body.

Stand straight with your shoulders back and your arms and hands out at your sides. Breathe. Fill your lungs and imagine you can begin to feel the front of your body. Starting with your forehead, bring your energy and awareness through your eyes, your nose and mouth, the front of your shoulders and chest, your stomach and the front of your legs and tops of your feet. Imagine you can put your full energy and attention on the front side of your body. If you feel any tension there, imagine you can breathe and release that tension now. If needed, you may run the palm of your hand down the front half of your body to increase your awareness of this area.

Next, beginning again with the top of your head, bring your awareness to the back of your head and neck, your shoulder blades, your spine and buttocks and the backs of your legs and soles of your feet. Breathe and focus on sending all your energy and awareness into the back side of your body. If needed, run your palms down your back and the backs of your legs. If you feel any tension there, imagine you can breathe and release that tension now.

Find peace within both the front and back of the body. Breathe into your entire body and exhale any tensions. When you're ready, bring your awareness back into the here and now.

•• ● ••
JOURNAL PROMPT
Movement within the Frontal Plane

How did it feel to focus on your body in that way? If guided, you could take a few notes.

1. How did the front side of your body feel?
2. How did your back side feel?

3. Were you able to release any tensions by drawing your awareness into these areas?

This is only the beginning of what you will experience with this
plane of motion. Bringing extra awareness to your body helps begin the
important work of grounding.

Movement within the Transverse Plane

The Transverse Plane divides the top half of your body from your legs.
The dividing line is right at your waist. If you've ever done sit-ups, the
Transverse Plane is that spot in your waist where you bend to touch
your toes. Especially with all the sitting most of us do these days, movement at the waist can be very energizing.

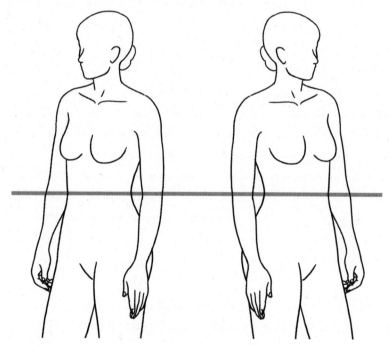

Image 2: Transverse Plane

• • ● • •
EXERCISE
Movement within the Transverse Plane

Stand with your feet flat on the floor and your hands out to your sides. Point your fingers down and relax your arms. Feel your arms hanging and imagine you can remove any residual tensions within them.

When you're ready, gently twist your body to the right and gaze over your right shoulder. Do this gently without forcing. When you're ready, swing back the other direction and gaze over your left shoulder.

Repeat this motion and allow your arms to swing freely as you move gently back and forth. Imagine you can feel the freedom of movement and this feeling brings you a sense of joy.

Continue for as long as you're guided. When you're ready, stop the movement and stand facing forward. Feel the blood circulating within the body. Allow yourself to feel the increased energy you stirred up through your gentle movements. Notice how this new awareness helps bring you greater energy and peace as you go about your day.

• • ● • •
JOURNAL PROMPT
Movement within the Transverse Plane

If you're guided, you can make notes about this exercise.

1. How did you feel when you began swinging your arms?
2. By gently moving and sending light into the body, did you feel increased energy when you finished the process?

Remember that this exercise doesn't need to be done for more than a couple of minutes. There's no right or wrong and it should not feel painful in any way. If you cannot look over your shoulder, just do the best you can to twist a little and know that over time with more movement, you may be able to do more.

Movement within the Sagittal Plane

For Ancestral Energy Healing, the most important of these three is the Sagittal Plane that divides your body into two halves, left and right. To think about this Sagittal Plane, you can use your imagination to envision an invisible line that runs from the top of your head, moves through your body, and cuts you in half at the base of your spine. Each half contains one of your arms, one of your legs, and each half of your face. This is an incredibly powerful plane you will work with later in this book. For now, you can do a simple movement exercise to connect with these two sides of yourself.

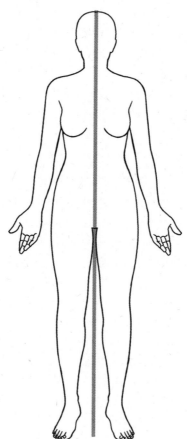

Image 3: Sagittal Plane

•• • ••
EXERCISE
Movement within the Sagittal Plane

Follow a few simple steps to get in touch with this powerful plane of motion within.

Stand upright with your feet flat on the floor. Begin with your right side and slowly lift your right arm, stretching it in front of you.

Circle your right arm overhead, slowly and deliberately. Count out a number of rotations you'd like to do. Any amount is okay. When this feels complete or you've done all you want, place your right arm by your side.

Next, when you're ready, lift your left arm over your head. Slowly circle your left arm deliberately with care, circling your arm around as many times as you wish. If possible, match the number on your left side with the rotations you already did on your right side to create greater balance. Complete this exercise and rest your left arm by your side.

Easy enough to do, yet powerful in helping you get in touch with your inner being and, ultimately, your ancestors. Keep in mind that you may have stiff shoulders or difficulty with this motion. If so, do your best and move with care and compassion for yourself.

•• • ••
JOURNAL PROMPT
Movement within the Sagittal Plane

Take a moment to make a few notes in your journal.

1. How did you feel rotating your right arm?
2. How did your left arm feel?
3. What differences did you sense in the energy between the two arms?

Taking a moment to consciously observe subtle changes in the two halves of your physical body can yield amazing results when you build on those sensations in your Ancestral Energy Healing practice.

Using Planes of Motion for Ancestral Energy Healing

How are you going to utilize the motion within your body to benefit and heal your ancestors? That's what we'll explore next. First, I must briefly share a little background about energy healing.

Energy healing recognizes the fact that you are much more than your physical body. Within you is an energetic component that cannot be seen, but is nevertheless very real. You could call this the soul. One of the best ways to sense the energetic self is when you're attending a funeral. Clearly, if you're in the presence of a loved one who has passed away, you see the physical body there, but the special animating force that made your loved one who they were in life is no more. That unseen aspect is quite real, and just like you would care for your physical body, the energy body also needs care and attention. Several methods have been created to help bring that balance to the energetic self, including the most popular healing modality, Reiki.

General energy healing typically involves using your inner vision to imagine yourself connecting with Universal Life Force (an abundant stream of light that flows down from the heavens) and sending that light out your hands into the energy field of another person or animal.

Because of the shifts in energy we're now experiencing around earth, I was clearly shown that these days, healing methods should begin by connecting to white light and sending that light through the top of the head, through the spine, and into the limbs while allowing the light to flow inside the body to make subtle changes from the inside out. This is the same kind of technique you used earlier in the guided imagery section.

The method differs from the old way energy healing was delivered because back in the days when people needed to get out of their bodies, as mentioned earlier, Reiki and other healing techniques required healers to send energy to the person from the outside, through the energetic fields that surround the body in hopes that doing so would make needed changes to the energy inside. Now, because of this critical need for grounding, the exact opposite is needed. Sending light and healing symbols through the interior of the body and having that light connect the crown chakra with the soles of the feet and earth helps people connect to earth and sky and be in their bodies.

Further, I was shown that each half of your body, divided along the Sagittal Plane, relates to one half of your lineage. In other words, one side represents your mother and her lineage, the other half represents your father and his lineage. This insight is something I've shared with students and clients alike with great results that you will be experiencing firsthand later in this book.

Before you can learn to do healing in this way, you must first determine which half of your body represents your biological mother's lineage and which half of your body represents your biological father's lineage. Earlier in the sections on past-life regression and Genealogical Regression, I mentioned that you may have any number of family configurations, and all those connections are important and valuable to your soul. It makes sense to send love, light, and healing to anybody who raised you or influenced your upbringing, whether they're related to you or not. That still holds true, yet in this upcoming exercise, you will be tuning in to your own physiology and biology. Whether you know your birth parents or not, you will be tuning in to their energy because things from your ancestral lineage are carried within your DNA. I found there is a way to tap into those areas and do a very specific energy healing process on the things you are carrying within your cells. You'll discover how to do this process by first using the art of Applied Kinesiology, also known as Muscle Testing. The term *Kinesiology* comes from Greek and means "study of motion."[17] Using Applied Kinesiology, you can not only determine challenged areas within your body, but you can also learn to receive binary guidance and yes-no answers about any number of issues you face.

---

17. Valentine, Valentine, and Hetrick, *Applied Kinesiology*, 2.

Tools for Muscle Testing

For the Ancestral Healing processes you'll be doing, you will use Muscle Testing to determine which side of your body relates to each set of ancestors.

Before we get into answering that question, I will give you a crash course on Muscle Testing in case this is new information for you. Even if you've done techniques like this before, an occasional review of the steps can be helpful for everyone, including myself.

Muscle Testing can be used to direct your actions, or to find out the truth and answers within yourself that will be for your highest good. It's important to note here that although you want to discover the *truth*, the truth is subjective. What may be the truth for you and for your best may not work for me. Everybody's different. The Muscle Testing process gauges what will work better for you as an individual, and at times, answers can vary as circumstances change. The easiest way to begin to find the best answers for you is to learn to craft statements.

Creating Positive Statements and Testing for Yes and No

Before you can begin your Muscle Testing practice, you must set some rules about how to proceed. All Muscle Testing is done by noting the strength of your body after making affirmative statements, so you will need to train yourself to make proper and affirmative statements and form proper questions. To become proficient in doing this, you must learn how to use the tools so they give you a definite visual or physical cue that represents both a *yes* and a *no* answer. I discovered saying my name is a good test because that's something I obviously know for certain that's not subject to change. To be fully clear with my Higher Self, I say, "In this lifetime, my name is Shelley." This statement should, obviously, receive a definite yes answer. I always say "in this lifetime" because you and I have had many names throughout the ages. That way the test is stronger and leaves little room for error, and I can visibly see my own strength in my body with whatever tool I'm using.

Next, to be fully clear and to make sure I am working in the correct manner, I ask a second question that I know for sure will result in a no answer, such as, "In this lifetime, my name is George." When I ask if my name is George, regardless of which tool I'm working with, I will obviously receive a no answer, which means my muscles will be weak. Once I have a clear connection with my Higher Self as to what a yes or a no looks like, so to speak, then I am ready to ask my more important set of questions with the expectation that I will accurately receive the yes and no responses I need to help me move forward accordingly.

Your Best Interest

Once you establish a yes or no, you will want to begin getting into what you wanted to ask about in the first place. To be effective at this, you need to set up proper positive statements to help you make your inquiries. The best phrase to use when you're beginning any questioning is this: "It is in my best interest." To date, I've never found anything better, and the statement about your best interest has proven to be a very powerful way to do these tests because the statement leaves less room for error. You can literally ask for clarity about any subject by beginning with that phrase. A few examples of positive statements include the following:

- It is in my best interest to drive to the beach today.
- It is in my best interest to eat this brand of multivitamin.
- It is in my best interest to apply for a job with XYZ Company.

The possibilities are endless. Let's explore our Muscle Testing tools and discuss how you would receive a yes or no or answer an important question with each of them.

• • ● • •

EXERCISE AND JOURNAL PROMPT
Practice Statements for Muscle Testing Your Best Interest

Take out your journal and create at least five positive statements: "It is in my best interest to _____."

Next, fill in the blanks. Make some of the statements things you know you can get a yes answer on, such as, "It is in my best interest to eat a balanced diet," or, "It is in my best interest to exercise," or, "...to take care of my health and wellness." You get the point.

Create more statements using things you know you can receive a no answer on. For example, "It is in my best interest to eat junk food every day," or, "...to skip brushing my teeth for a week." Those are silly examples, of course, but think of something that would definitely give you a no answer.

Continue to use your imagination to create more statements where you do not know the answer in advance. The example I gave about working for XYZ Company is a good one. Pick something you want to know but that does not have a solid yes or no answer.

Think of other positive statements and note those. Craft statements that you know have a no or negative answer. Begin to feel in the body how these two states of being differ and make notes on those subtle energies.

Put the list aside for later when you're doing your practicing with your chosen Muscle Testing tool. Keep the list with you to use as a standard of comparison when we do further Ancestral Energy Healing exercises later in the book.

Tools of the Trade

I'd like to share a few of the many items you can use for Applied Kinesiology or Muscle Testing that will help you learn more about yourself. There are so many ways to do this; here are three of my favorites:

- **Pendulum**—Using a rock on a rope and training it to give yes or no answers.
- **Fingers**—By looping your thumb and index finger together and testing the strength or by pressing your index fingers together.
- **Object**—Testing the strength of your arm by holding it out straight and attempting to lift a simple object.

We'll review each of these tools in the next few sections and I will share how you will use them for Muscle Testing.

Muscle Testing with a Pendulum

One of my personal favorite tools is the pendulum. What is a pendulum, you ask? I like to call it a rock on a rope. That's my personal joke. In reality, a pendulum is a chain or string with a weighted object on the end that helps you get in touch with your subconscious mind and Higher Self. Usually, pendulums are made with silver chains with gemstone points on one end and a heavier bead on the other that you hold in your hand. While it theoretically doesn't look like much, when properly programmed and trained, your pendulum can help you answer all the toughest questions you have in life. Be sure you pick a pendulum you love, meaning you love the stone on it and the chain, the weight of the pendulum, and so forth, then have fun experimenting.

Finding Yes or No with Your Pendulum

Before you can use the pendulum to help answer the big questions, you must train it to give you a yes or no answer. There are a couple of ways to do this and no right or wrong. Still, you must learn to positively identify when the pendulum is telling you yes verses no so you can move forward with confidence that you're uncovering the material you most need at any given time. There are typically two ways your pendulum will signal a yes or no. For me, I hold the beaded end of the chain between my fingers and notice that the yes answer is a clockwise spinning and no is signified by a counterclockwise spinning. That may or may not work for you.

Another way many people train the pendulum is to use a circular chart marked with a Yes and No. I've included a chart for you here. The chart helps you train your pendulum to signify a yes answer when it swings back and forth vertically, and the no answer is shown when the pendulum swings along the horizontal axis. Try that. See if it works for you.

One suggestion I have is this: I don't like to force these things. I prefer and recommend you treat your pendulum training process as a phase of getting to know yourself better. Rather than forcing your subconscious mind into submission by telling it what to do and demanding your pendulum swing a certain way, I've always found it's better for me when I allow the subconscious mind to show me how it wants to express the answers. Likewise, you may find this chart is of no use to you at all. If not, that's fine. Try another way. I simply offer it here to help you, even though I've always found charts to be harder to use. Once I started practicing with my pendulums for a while, I found the clockwise or counterclockwise rotations were always easier for me. You may be just the opposite. As I said, you get to know yourself better by experimenting to see what you like better. I suggest trying them both, and then using whichever is easier. Why make life more difficult than it needs to be? The pendulum is an extension of your subconscious mind, so I've found that if you want to get in better rapport and alignment with who you really are, doing what comes easy is a great policy to follow.

Do what you do and allow yourself to express in the way that feels most authentic to who you truly are as a soul. That's really the whole reason why we're doing this in the first place, to help get to know ourselves. There's no right or wrong here. The better you gain this alignment with your true self, the better your answers will be in the end because you will be allowing yourself the luxury of being truly who you are, and that's amazing.

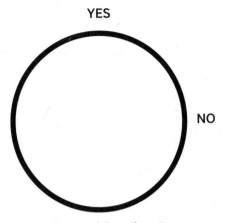

Image 4: Pendulum Chart #1

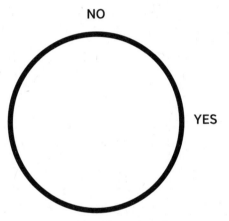

Image 5: Pendulum Chart #2

Use the charts to train your pendulum by holding the chain of your pendulum between your index finger and thumb and asking yes-no questions. While you do that, you will wait to see which direction the pendulum swings when you ask a question that has a definite yes answer. Then you will ask another question you know will receive a no answer and see which direction your pendulum swings.

It's important to keep in mind that in all spiritual practice, there's no right or wrong in how you receive the information. This is especially true with pendulums. The pendulum is a tool that helps you get in touch with the deepest aspects of yourself. Paying attention to the direction your pendulum wants to swing naturally begins the process of helping you tune in to your soul.

Also remember that at first, you may not see much of a swing at all. Keep working with it and trying this and know that over time, it will begin to swing more as you train yourself. Above all, enjoy this journey of self-discovery.

Training Your Pendulum

Once you train your pendulum to give yes or no answers, you're ready to begin asking more complex questions by testing affirmative statements and allowing those truths to emerge from the depths of the soul. To begin, we must ask questions that are super easy to ascertain the yes or no answers, and from there, we will eventually move to more challenging information.

•• ● ••
EXERCISE
Training Your Pendulum

To practice working with your pendulum, follow these simple steps.

Hold the chain or rope on your pendulum between your thumb and index finger on your dominant hand, or whichever hand feels most comfortable to you. Make the following statement: "My name is (state your name)." Wait to receive a yes answer.

Make a second statement: "My name is (state a name other than your own)." Wait to receive your no answer.

Pull out the list of "it is in my best interest" statements you made earlier. Practice reading those statements and phrases: "It is in my best interest to _____."

Go through each statement and wait for a yes or no. Trust what you receive.

Keep trying if you find it challenging at first. The swing may be minimal, but with time and patience, your answers will become clearer.

•• ● ••
JOURNAL PROMPT
Training Your Pendulum

If guided, make a few notes about your progress.

1. Which direction works best for you to receive a yes answer?
2. Which direction creates the best version of a no answer?
3. After practicing, did you find this exercise gets easier?

If you're not seeing strong results at first, keep practicing. Using the pendulum is like any sport or activity you do. Practice helps and improvement can happen in time. The pendulum can be a lot of fun to use, so enjoy the journey.

Muscle Testing with Your Fingers

Using a pendulum is amazing when you have one available, but what are you going to do if your trusted advisor isn't around? Another option for Muscle Testing is to use the power of your own fingers to tap into your soul and receive the yes or no answers you need. There are many ways to do this, so let's review the two that I've found most effective.

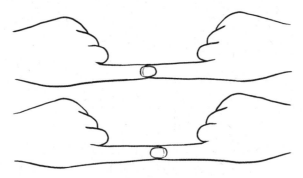

Image 6: Muscle Testing with the
Tips of Your Index Fingers

Muscle Testing with the Tips of Your Index Fingers

One of my favorite ways to do Muscle Testing is with the tips of my index fingers. The reason why I love this method so much is because I can do this anytime, anywhere, and with subtlety so people don't necessarily know what I'm doing even if they observe me in action. Because Muscle Testing is based on using strength in your body, you can use your index fingers by pointing them at each other and placing the fingernail of one of your fingers over the fingernail of the other. Then, when you ask the questions, you will either receive a strong magnetic pull that keeps your fingers together (yes or affirmative), or your fingers won't stay together at all (no or negative). It's fun, easy to do, and so helpful to use anytime, anywhere.

•• ● ••
EXERCISE
Muscle Testing with the Tips of Your Index Fingers

Here are the simple steps you can use to try this technique for yourself.

Hold your hands out in front of you and point your index fingers toward each other.

Place the tip of one of your index fingers on top of the fingernail on the index finger of your opposite hand so your two fingernails are lined up. I always put the tip of my left index finger on top of my right index fingernail. My dominant hand is my right, and this feels better to me. Everybody's different though, so try this both ways and see which feels more comfortable for you. Remember always that this is your journey, so do what feels right to you.

Once you've established your own best practice, imagine feeling a strong connection between your fingers. Make the following statement: "In this lifetime, my name is (state your name)." When you state your correct name, you should notice that when you try to pull your fingers apart or away from each other, they will stay together and strong. Continue practicing that until you receive a solid yes or affirmative answer.

Next, state the following: "My name is (some name other than your own)." Your fingers should pull apart easily when you make a false statement.

Continue practicing until you receive a solid no answer, meaning your fingers will not be strong and will not stay together.

When you're ready, make a statement about something you want to inquire about that demands either a yes or no answer and make the statement by saying the following: "It is in my best interest to _____."

Receive your yes or no answer and trust what you receive. For fun, you might want to practice this out in public at a grocery store or while you're with other people. Do it discreetly and you will see what I mean. People won't know you're asking questions and yet you can receive inner guidance anytime, anywhere. It's a lot of fun.

This technique is easy to do. That said, like any of these ideas, you get better as you practice, so if you didn't feel the sensations in the hands as strongly as you wanted, know that you can become more proficient with it over time.

·· ● ··
JOURNAL PROMPT
Muscle Testing with the Tips of Your Index Fingers

Consider making notes about your progress.

1. Can you feel the strength of the connection between your fingers when receiving the yes answer?
2. How easily do your fingers pull apart when creating a no response?

I've been doing a lot more Muscle Testing with the tips of my index fingers these days because by using my own fingers, I won't have to go out and find anything. Whether you're in the grocery store or at work, this one is good to use anytime. Try it.

Muscle Testing with a Finger Loop

There's one more fun way to Muscle Test with your fingers that you may like better: using a finger loop. Similar to the index finger technique, you can once again use the inherent power within your own body to receive yes and no answers to simple questions by creating a loop with your fingers. The easiest and strongest way to do this is by pressing the tip of your index finger to the tip of your thumb. Like the fingernail method, this can also be done discreetly, and you can take this with you to use anytime, anywhere. Either hand is okay to use for this. I use my right hand most of the time, but again, practice to see what you like best. Once you put your index finger and thumb together, you practice asking questions you know will yield either the yes or no answer and see what information you receive. The reason I use my index finger rather than one of the others is because it's typically the strongest to use. Again though, if you feel called to use your middle or ring finger and press that against your thumb instead, go for it. As always, this is your process, your journey. Let's take a closer look at that now.

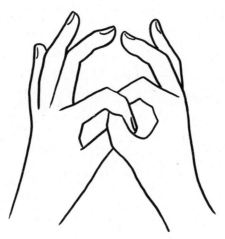

Image 7: Muscle Testing with a Finger Loop

•• • ••
EXERCISE
Muscle Testing with a Finger Loop

To try another way to do Muscle Testing with your fingers, follow these steps.

Create a loop by placing the tip of your index finger (or finger of your choice) to the tip of your thumb on whichever hand you feel more comfortable using. Take your other hand and make a loop with your index (or other) finger and thumb and connect them in the middle of your other fingers so they are joined.

Make the following statement: "In this lifetime, my name is (state your name)." Try pulling your fingers apart. They should stay together and be strong. Continue practicing that until you receive a solid yes answer.

Next, state the following: "My name is (some name other than your own)." Pull your fingers apart and notice how easily that happens when stating something false. Continue to practice receiving no answers.

When you're ready, ask about something you'd like to know by making a statement that requires a yes or no answer and saying, "It is in my best interest to _____." Notice whether you receive a yes or no. Trust what you receive.

Trusting the answer is so important to your success with any kind of Muscle Testing. When you trust yourself at this deepest level, over time, that's part of what makes this easier to do. You gain a lot of credibility and confidence with the one person who matters most—you. That wonderful relationship you establish with yourself helps create better interactions with everybody you meet, and you can act in accordance with what is truly best for you. Remember to take your time and allow the process to become easier as you go along.

•• ● ••
JOURNAL PROMPT
Muscle Testing with a Finger Loop

Make note of your progress with this technique.

1. Did you find the finger loop easier than the others or more difficult?

2. Could you differentiate the strength of the positive and negative answers?

3. After practicing, do you prefer this method to the others or not?

Continue to practice until you feel comfortable getting the yes or no and trusting the answers, and above all, have fun.

Muscle Testing with an Object

Another way to do Muscle Testing is to use the strength of your own arm by holding an object while making affirmative statements. There are several kinds of objects you could use for this purpose. I recommend trying out different objects to see how they feel in your hand. Find one you like best then use that same item every time you do a muscle test. The more you use your special object that you've assigned to this purpose, the more consistent the results.

Image 8: Muscle Testing with an Object

I've used aluminum whistling kettles, coffee cups, and all sorts of other items before finally settling on my favorite object, which is a metal trivet (used for placing hot items on a table). I like the trivet because it's heavier than the teakettle I used to use. The reason a heavier object may work best is because your conscious mind, waking or ego self, will have no room to doubt what you're experiencing. The yes answers you'll receive will make this heavier object light as a feather, no matter how heavy it actually feels, and if you're getting a no answer, your object will feel like a lead bowling ball. Please know that you may find you like a lighter object better, and that's fine. Experiment with different items until you find the one you like best.

When I do this exercise, I grasp the item in my hand, hold my dominant arm out straight, and use my arm strength to test for a yes or no answer. I've found that using the dominant arm helps in receiving the most accurate results. You may find you're different though, so experiment with this and do whatever feels best. As with all Muscle Testing tools, if you make a statement that receives a yes response, your muscles will be strong, and you will be able to easily lift your object from the table. If you're making a statement that receives a no answer, your arm will feel too weak, and the object will feel too heavy to lift. Let's do an exercise to see how this works.

•• ● ••
EXERCISE
Muscle Testing with an Object

Test for a yes and no by following these simple steps.

Take out your testing object and grasp it with your fingers while holding your arm out straight with the object lying on a table or another flat surface. State the following: "In this lifetime, my name is (state your name)."

If your arm lifts easily, which it should, you've received your yes response. Continue holding the object in your hand and keep your arm straight while saying the following: "In this lifetime, my name is (say any name other than your own)." As you make that statement and say the other name, try to lift your arm. You should not be able to lift your hand from the table. That heavy response signifies your no answer. This is a fascinating method to try because even if you held a feather, you would not be able to lift your arm because you're making a statement that is not true. Once you notice your arm will not lift, make a note that you have succeeded in noticing a negative or no answer.

Ask other questions by pulling out the list you made earlier and stating, "It is in my best interest to _____." Keep practicing. Know that you can improve over time.

•• ● ••

JOURNAL PROMPT
Muscle Testing with an Object

Now that you've worked through that process, if you'd like, make some notes.

1. Did you enjoy the object Muscle Testing process?
2. Could you sense the difference in weight between the affirmative and negative answers?
3. How hard was it to lift something when you received a no?

This is an awesome method to use because the weight gives you an undeniable sensation of the positive result. That said, you may not always have the luxury of being in a place where you have objects to lift. That's why it helps to know several methods.

My hope is by practicing and trying out all the methods, you will find the one that works best for you that you will enjoy doing the most. Life needs to be enjoyable, so take some time to discover one or two methods you like. Once you figure that out, use that technique and enjoy. Consider which one seems both easy and convenient. There's no right or wrong. Using what works for you is best, and that differs for everybody.

Muscle Testing to Discover
Ancestral Lineage within Your Body

Once you feel confident that your Muscle Testing process is going well and you are getting accurate answers with whichever technique you enjoy best, you can use your newfound skill to determine which side of your body represents your mother's side of the family and which half of your body carries your father's ancestral heritage. All the exercises and journeys we will take for the remainder of the book will depend on your answer to that question.

· · ● · ·
EXERCISE
Muscle Testing to
Discover Ancestral Lineage within Your Body

Ancestral Energy Healing supposes that within your physical body, you carry the energy of your ancestors. Acknowledging the body is split in two—the right side and the left side—you will create questions and use your Muscle Testing skills to find the answers.

When you're ready, pull out your pendulum or engage with whichever Muscle Testing technique worked best for you. That may involve using an object or simply Muscle Testing with your fingers or a finger loop.

Be sure you pick the technique that you enjoyed the most. Enjoying what you're doing is so important. The more you enjoy the journey, the better and the more likely you are to receive the best answers. Remember nobody's the same, so do what's easy and what you love.

To receive the information, there are four statements you will make using your Muscle Testing strategy:

My mother's lineage is represented by the right side of my body.

My mother's lineage is represented by the left side of my body.

My father's lineage is represented by the right side of my body.

My father's lineage is represented by the left side of my body.

After stating each sentence aloud, receive the answer. Write the answer down in your journal—yes or no for each. Repeat until you've answered all four.

This should result in clarity about which side of your body represents your mother and which side represents your father. If you are not quite clear, try again or wait for our next exercise in the chapter on guided imagery journeys.

Aside from dividing your body in half, another important place to explore within your body is your teeth. There is a long-held belief that your karma is tied to your teeth.[18] When I first heard that idea, I assumed that meant karma from past lives, but now I've come to understand that the upper and lower sets of teeth can represent your mother's and father's lineages. You can use Muscle Testing to inquire about your teeth and how they relate to your ancestral lineages by using the following four statements:

My mother's lineage is represented by my upper teeth.
My mother's lineage is represented by my lower teeth.
My father's lineage is represented by my upper teeth.
My father's lineage is represented by my lower teeth.

After stating each sentence aloud, receive the yes or no answer. Repeat until you've completed all four.

Like the process of determining your lineage along the Sagittal Plane, where your teeth are concerned, there is no one-size-fits-all answer to that question. My students and clients reported varying answers. Some said their father was represented in the top set while their mother was embodied in their lower teeth and vice versa. Test this for yourself and note your answer.

•• ● ••

JOURNAL PROMPT
Muscle Testing to
Discover Ancestral Lineage within Your Body

Take a moment and record the following alongside the answers you already received.

1. Were you able to get an answer as to which side of the body and which teeth represent which family members?

2. Were you surprised by what you uncovered?

3. Did you try more than one technique to receive answers?

---

18. Steiner, *Karmic Relationships*, 29, 40.

You may feel pressured now to come up with the perfect answer about which side of your body represents which parent using this method. If you practice this and find Muscle Testing or pendulums are not your thing and you do not resonate with this way of receiving information, don't worry. Coming up in the next chapter, you will have a chance to discover those answers in a different way using guided imagery journeys. Before we do that, let's revisit the planes of motion exercises with your new knowledge in mind.

Ancestral Healing with the Frontal Plane

Earlier we discussed the Frontal Plane, the line that separates the front of your body, including your face, chest, stomach, and so forth, from the back of your body.

In the Ancestral Healing process, now that you've learned which side of your body holds the energy of your mother's and father's lineages, you will use that information to divide your physical body up by the left and right sides. With the Frontal Plane, the front of your body can be used then to represent the future and the future generations to who you may dedicate this important work of Ancestral Healing, and the back of your body can be used to represent the ancestors who lived before you and all the energies that existed prior to your birth.

When you think of this, it makes sense, right? Facing forward in the direction of your future. Things behind you are in the past. In healing, you can perform some easy exercises to assist both the ancestors of the past and these future generations.

•• • ••
EXERCISE
Ancestral Healing with the Frontal Plane

Stand upright with your feet flat on the floor. Think about the back of your body—your head, your back, and the backs of your legs. As you do, send love and light to all your ancestors who have come before you.

Next, think of the front side of your body—your forehead, face, chest, knees, and legs. As you do, send love and healing light to all future generations of your family.

That's it. We will do more extensive healing later, but for now, you just completed a powerful Ancestral Healing process.

•• ● ••
JOURNAL PROMPT
Ancestral Healing with the Frontal Plane

Take a moment to note the following:

1. How did you feel acknowledging your ancestral past and future generations?

2. Did you feel you made an impact on the future of your family?

3. Record any other thoughts or feelings you had during the process.

This is so easy to do and yet so powerful for honoring your entire clan.

Ancestral Healing with the Transverse Plane

The Transverse Plane, as you recall, divides your body at the hips. There are several movement disciplines such as Qigong that actively engage this plane of motion to create restorative balance to the body. In this exercise, you will do exactly what you did earlier in the book, only this time, you will bring the conscious awareness of the ancestors within you into your every movement.

•• ● ••
EXERCISE
Ancestral Healing with the Transverse Plane

Stand with your feet flat on the floor about hip distance apart. Put your arms out to your sides. Allow your hands to hang in a relaxed manner. Gently twist your body to the right and gaze over your right shoulder. Do this gently without forcing.

When you're ready, swing back the other direction and gaze over your left shoulder. Continue moving side to side. Bring conscious awareness into the movement.

Twist five times to the right (or any number of times you choose and feel comfortable doing) while thinking of the ancestor and family line that is associated with your right side based on your Muscle Testing exercise.

Next, swing the same number times to the left and consciously consider the other side of your family and the lineage that side represents, all while swinging freely and relaxing. Continue moving as guided and when you're ready, pause. Feel a sense of movement and relaxation within you.

This process is so easy to do. Movement of any kind can be incredibly beneficial for your physical, mental, and emotional well-being.

•• • ••
JOURNAL PROMPT
Ancestral Healing with the Transverse Plane

Consider the following questions.

1. Consider the exercise you did earlier in the book and recall how you felt.

2. Once you brought your energy and attention to the ancestors, could you feel a difference between your right and left sides?

3. How so? Describe how each side felt in comparison to the other.

Make note of any other sensations or thoughts that occurred to you during this range of motion exercise.

Ancestral Healing with the Sagittal Plane

Although we will do much more work on the Sagittal Plane in our next chapter, for now, it's helpful to repeat the earlier exercise while bringing the awareness of your lineage to the forefront of your mind.

•• ● ••

EXERCISE
Ancestral Healing with the Sagittal Plane

Stand upright. Lift and circle your right arm. While rotating your right arm slowly, bring the awareness of which side of the family your right arm represents into your mind.

When you're ready, stop and switch, rotating your left arm with this same ancestral consciousness. Do these motions at least three times on each side of the body, so long as that feels comfortable to you.

Enjoy the process and allow yourself to continue to open to new energies and awareness as you go.

•• ● ••

JOURNAL PROMPT
Ancestral Healing with the Sagittal Plane

If you'd like, consider the following and note this in your journal.

1. How does this new awareness of your ancestors make you feel?

2. What differences did you sense in the right and left sides of your body?

3. Make note of any other thoughts or ideas that emerged during this process.

Thoughts are things and they exist within our energy fields. Once you begin consciously moving with ancestors in mind, you may find new thoughts and ideas emerge. Be sure and make note of anything remarkable.

Grounding to the Earth

You've been on a journey to connect and to become more grounded. Nothing connects us more with each other and with those who paved the way for us than grounding to the earth. Grounding is easy enough to do when you take a few moments out of your day to walk barefoot on the earth and call forth to your ancestors. They shared the same soil as us. They once walked in familiar places and considering that from time to time is a wonderful tribute to your lineage and all who helped you on the path of life. On that note, let's do an exercise to get you in a grounded state of being. For ease, you may want to record this journey.

•• ● ••
EXERCISE
Grounding to the Earth

Sit in a comfortable chair with your hands in your lap and feet flat on the floor. Close your eyes. Breathe. Take a deep, healing breath in through your nose, breathing in love and peace and light. Exhale tensions and concerns.

Imagine a beautiful beam of pure white light coming down through the top of your head. Feel that light moving through your head and forehead, floating into your eyes, your nose, your mouth, and your jaw, moving down, down, down, into your neck and shoulders, into your arms, your elbows, your wrists, your hands and fingertips.

Feel the light as it continues flowing down, down, down through your shoulders, flowing down your spine into your heart center. Feel your heart energy expand as the light continues to move down into your stomach, through your torso to the base of your spine, and into your legs, flowing into your thighs, your knees, your calves, your ankles and heels and down into the soles of your feet and into your toes.

Imagine the light is getting stronger now as it flows from your head, through your body, and into your legs and feet. Imagine you can feel the soles of your feet tingling beneath you and allow that loving light to extend beyond your feet and travel into the earth. Feel an invisible cord of light moving from the bottom of your feet through the floors of your space, through the many layers of the earth, flowing down, down, down into the earth until you are fully connected with the iron core of Mother Earth. Take your time to feel this connection.

Pause here.

Allow any tensions you carry within your body to flow down through this energetic cord of light and travel deep within Mother Earth. Allow Mother Earth to relieve you of any stress and know that as you release any stressful energy, Mother Earth uses and transforms that energy into a loving, healing, and nourishing light for the earth.

Keep this connection you feel with the earth as you bring your awareness back into your body, fully aligning with the deep grounded and centered feeling of your new connection with Mother Earth. Know that wherever you are, this is your place in the world. You are connected to this home and place, and you know that here, all is well.

Take a deep breath in through your nose and allow yourself to become completely relaxed and totally connected with Mother Earth. Allow the supportive energies of Mother Earth to move through every single cell of your being. As you do, breathe in the energy of joy, peace, and happiness as you inhale, and exhale love and light. Very good.

Filled with peaceful light, feeling better than you did before, know that in a moment, when you count from five, you will come back into the room, feeling awake, refreshed, and better than you felt before.

Five—grounded, centered, and balanced. Four—continuing to process this new grounded energy and earth connection in your dreams tonight so by tomorrow morning, you will be fully integrated into your connection with Mother Earth. Three—keeping your connection with Mother Earth, you are constantly grounded, centered, and balanced. You will drive carefully and be safe in all activities. Two—you're grounded, centered, and balanced, and one—you're back.

•• • ••
JOURNAL PROMPT
Grounding to the Earth

Take a moment to make notes about any sensations you experienced during that exercise.

1. How did it feel to be fully grounded to the core of the earth?

2. In the coming days, practice keeping that connection and make note of how you feel.

3. If needed, reestablish that connection to Mother Earth. Notice if the process becomes easier.

4. What benefits or changes do you notice within yourself by making a more conscious connection with your home and the place you're living right now?

5. How can you benefit from this deepening of the earth connection as you move forward on your journey through life?

People need a sense of place and more than ever, we need to be grounded. I truly believe that if each of us would make a more conscious effort to go outside and put our hands on our wonderful Mother Earth, we would feel better, and that would translate into greater peace and happiness in all aspects of our lives. To further the progress from that exercise, go outside. Hug a tree, put your bare feet in the ground, and feel that connection. Try it and keep the momentum going.

Summing Up

The work of Ancestral Healing is a monumental task that requires various levels of consciousness to complete. By actively acknowledging the role the ancestors have within your body, you can begin to move and act on behalf of your lineage and create greater light and healing within your family tree without uncovering deep emotions and feelings that may emerge from guided imagery journeys. Likewise, by recognizing and honoring the inherent connection we have to the earth and our need for grounding, we can shift our consciousness. Actively taking care of the planet for future generations can assist with the journey of Ancestral Energy Healing and reap benefits for decades to come.

Chapter Eight
Ancestral Energy Healing

The beginning of this book explored the numerous legitimate scientific studies regarding the field of epigenetics and DNA that prove the things that happened to our ancestors—be they mind, body, or spirit related—are affecting us in the here and now. This groundbreaking information suggests that because that is the case, you and I might be feeling the pains of our ancestors within our bodies. You also learned to use your own strength to discover important information about your ancestors and lineage. For some people, movement or Muscle Testing works wonders. Others find guided imagery journeys work better to help them connect with ancestors and loved ones. We're all different.

In this chapter, you will build on the material you did with embodied exercises and take journeys to help you release and heal any unwanted influences within your own body in hopes of achieving greater peace, happiness, and joy in your current life. By healing those influences, you no longer carry the energies of the past with you so future generations can ultimately benefit from this deeper work. All exercises in this chapter will be easier if you take the time to record them in advance.

Discover Your Ancestors within You

First, building on the work you did with the Sagittal Plane in the previous chapter, you will go on a guided journey to meet with the Higher Selves of your biological parents and determine which side of your body represents which set of ancestors. Remember that you will be addressing the soul essence of your parents. That's important because you may not know them if you were adopted or raised by caregivers other than your parents. That's okay. You can still invite them to join you. Likewise, if there is still forgiveness work to be done with your biological parents, you may want to skip this for now if you find it difficult to connect with them solely on an energetic level. That's where your Muscle Testing practice can be a true gift. You can trust the strength within your body and use that to find your answers without going through emotions that may be too challenging. The journey is yours and you can do this when and how you would like. The connection here will be deeply energizing, and if there were any doubts before as to which side of your body is which, you will receive clarity and added healing after you go through this experience.

•• ● ••

EXERCISE
Discover Your Ancestors within You

Sit in a comfortable chair with your hands in your lap and feet flat on the floor. Close your eyes. Breathe. Take a deep, healing breath in through your nose, breathing in love and peace and light. Exhale any tensions and concerns. Continue to breathe, and as you do, you find yourself becoming more and more relaxed. Feel the breath going into your body. Imagine you are breathing in love, and joy, and relaxation, and peace, and you continue to exhale tensions and concerns. Very good. Continue to breathe and count as you do so, noticing that as you count and breathe, your state of inner peace is relaxing more and more.

Breathing in peace, joy, and love and exhaling tensions. Continue to breathe. With each breath you take, you are becoming more and more relaxed. Find yourself breathing in peace, joy, and love as you release tensions and concerns.

Go ahead now and imagine a beautiful beam of pure white light coming down through the top of your head. Feel that light moving through your head and forehead, floating into your eyes, your nose, your mouth, and your jaw.

Continue to breathe as the light moves down, down, down, down, through your neck and shoulders, into your arms, your elbows, your wrists, your hands, and fingertips.

Feel the light as it continues flowing down, down, down into your shoulders, your collarbone, your shoulder blades, and continues to flow down, down, down, into your heart center. Feel your heart's energy expand as the light continues to move down into your stomach, traveling down, down, down your spine and into your lungs, flowing down to the base of your spine. Continue to breathe as this loving light moves down, down, down, through the base of your spine, flowing into your legs—your thighs, your knees, your calves, your ankles and heels, and down into the soles of your feet and into your toes.

Imagine the light is getting stronger now as it moves from the crown of your head, all the way down through your body, through your spine, through your legs and down and out the soles of your feet. The light is becoming stronger now, so strong, it begins to pour out of your heart center, creating a beautiful golden ball of light that surrounds you by about three feet in all directions. Imagine feeling yourself floating inside this peaceful golden ball of light. Know that within this golden ball of light, you are safe, secure, and totally carefree, and know that within the golden light, only that which is of your highest good can come through.

Imagine there's a doorway in front of you. You can see the door, feel the door, or just have an inner knowing the door is there. When you count back from three, you will walk through that door and go inside a beautiful room, a sacred space where you can feel totally relaxed, nurtured, and protected. Ready? Three, two, one; you're opening the door. Open the door now and walk or float inside your beautiful room. Allow this place to fill your body with light and energy. Become fully refreshed and energized.

Pause here.

As you continue to enjoy your sacred space, imagine your loving angel, guide, or being of light is floating down to join you now. Feel them land right next to you and imagine they are with you right now. Feel the immense unconditional love they have for you. Know that they are here to support you in this journey.

Take a moment to let your guide know that today you would like to discover which side of your body represents your mother's ancestors and which side of your body represents your father's. Take your time and speak with your guide about your intentions and allow them to give you any feedback.

Pause here.

When you're ready, imagine you can turn your attention to the other side of the room. There's a doorway there, and that door is opening now, and here come your mother and father. Know that these are their Higher Selves, the highest aspects of their souls, or their soul essences who are here with you. Imagine in this place, your mother and father are in perfect health, completely vital, and notice now that at a soul level they both love you unconditionally. Take a moment to say hello and receive this unconditional love.

Pause here.

Very nice. Now imagine you can speak with your mother's soul essence. Ask her to walk over to you and hold one of your hands, the hand that represents her and her ancestors and the entire family lineage on her side of the family.

Pause here.

Very nice. As you hold her hand, imagine you can ask her whether your upper or lower teeth represent her side of the family. Notice her answer. Allow her to share any explanations or have any discussion you would like.

Now imagine your father's soul essence can walk or float over to you. Your father is going to hold the other hand. Imagine he can let you know that the hand he is holding represents him, his ancestors, and the entire family lineage on his side of the family. Allow him to confirm whether your upper or lower teeth represent his lineage within your body. Allow him to share any other important information with you.

Pause here.

Continue holding your parents' hands for a moment. Feel what you feel within your body as your mother holds the hand that corresponds to her family. Then turn your attention to the hand your father is holding. Feel what you feel regarding your father's lineage. Take your time to speak with your parents about anything they wish to talk to you about today.

Pause here.

When you're ready, thank your parents for joining you today and giving you this valuable information. Imagine they can say goodbye for now. Feel that unconditional love they have for you and notice now that they both walk or float back through the door they came through. Know that you will see them again soon.

Take a moment to ask your guide for any further clarity or insights you need about this healing or the information you received today.

Pause here.

When you're finished, imagine you can thank your guide for being here today and watch your guide float up, up, up, floating back to where they came from. Know that you will see your guide again soon.

Take a deep breath in through your nose. Allow yourself to become completely relaxed inside your sacred space. Allow the supportive energies of your sacred space to move through every single cell of your being. Filled with peaceful light, feeling better than you did before, go ahead and turn around now and walk back through the door you came through and go back out to where you began your journey. Be there now, back where you began. Close that door behind you and know you will be back there again very soon.

In a moment, when you count from five, you will come back into the room, feeling awake, refreshed, and better than you did before.

Five—grounded, centered, and balanced. Four—continuing to process this new energy in your dreams tonight so by tomorrow morning, you will be fully integrated into these new insights. Three—still surrounded by that beautiful golden ball of light, knowing only that which is of your highest good can come through, you will find yourself driving carefully and being careful in all activities. Two—grounded, centered, and balanced, and one—you're back.

•• ● ••
JOURNAL PROMPT
Discover Your Ancestors within You

Having hopefully received important information about your lineage, take a moment to write some notes in your journal.

1. Were you able to meet with your parents' Higher Selves?
2. Which side of your body and which teeth are associated with your mother's lineage?
3. Which side of your body and which teeth represent your father's side of the family?
4. Were you surprised by what you discovered?
5. Make notes about any information your parents and your guide shared that you want to recall later.

This is a fascinating journey to take. My students all had completely different experiences with these processes and no two people gave the same answers. There is no one-size-fits-all in terms of which side of your body represents your mother's and your father's ancestors or which teeth carry your ancestral energy. This is something each person must explore individually. What you discover is perfect for you. We are all such unique aspects of creation, so honor that within yourself.

If you found the answer you received surprising, that might give you pause. Several students said they weren't sure what they received the first time was correct because the answer was so different than what they'd expected. For that reason, and also to help you begin to open up to the deep healing you can receive from this experience, you will go again on a second journey to gain greater clarity and begin to tune in to the ancestral energy within.

Deeper Healing with the Family

Next, whenever you are guided to do so, you will return to that same space, only this time, you will deepen your focus on each side of the body as it relates to your family. If the first experience surprised you, this second journey will hopefully clarify things for you. The exercise will be the same, only this time, you will go a bit further.

•• ● ••
EXERCISE
Deeper Healing with the Family

Retreat to your comfortable space. Breathe. With each breath you take, you are becoming more and more relaxed. Find yourself breathing in peace, joy, and love as you release tensions and concerns.

Feel a beautiful beam of pure white light coming down through the top of your head. Allow the light to move down, down, down, down, through your head, neck, and shoulders, into your arms, through your body and legs and down and out the soles of your feet.

Imagine the light is getting stronger now and begins to pour out of your heart center, creating a beautiful golden ball of light that surrounds you by about three feet in all directions. Imagine feeling yourself floating inside this peaceful golden ball of light. Know that within this golden ball of light, you are safe, secure, and totally carefree, and know that within the golden light, only that which is of your highest good can come through.

Walk through the door and go inside your beautiful room and imagine your loving guide is floating down to join you now. Feel them land right next to you and imagine they are with you right now. Feel the immense unconditional love they have for you. Know that they are here to support you in this journey.

Take a moment now to explain that you would like to meet with your parents' Higher Selves again to receive more information and clarity about the ancestral energies within your body.

Pause here.

When you're ready, notice the door you observed before. That door is opening, and your parents are coming through that door now. Remember these are their soul essences and feel the unconditional love they have for you. They're both happy to see you today.

Imagine you can speak to one of your parents. Ask them to move forward and take the hand that represents their family lineage. As you reach out and they hold your hand, if there is any uncertainty on your part that this is truly the correct side of your body that represents their lineage, allow them to speak with you about this until you can gain absolute clarity.

Pause here.

As you tune in to the feeling of the hand your parent is holding, go ahead now and scan your body. Beginning with the top of your head, feel and sense the energy moving down that side of your body, through your forehead, the eye on that side, the side of your nose, mouth, and jaw. Bring your focus to the arm on that side—your elbow, wrist, hand, and fingers. Scan your body and notice the shoulder on that side, your rib cage, your lung, your hip, leg, and foot. Imagine you notice any tensions or injuries you've had there, and you can also notice places that feel good. Notice all you can as you allow yourself to tune in to the idea that the energy on this side of your body is relating to your ancestors. You can also notice the teeth that relate to that parent and imagine sensing a tremendous flow of energy moving through either your upper or lower teeth as they relate to that parent and their lineage. Allow this healing to fill you with light and peace.

Pause here.

When you're ready, allow that parent to release your hand and step aside while your other parent approaches you. Imagine your other parent moves forward and takes the hand that represents their family lineage. As you reach out and they hold your hand, if there is any uncertainty that this is truly the correct side of your body that represents their lineage, allow them to speak with you about this until you can gain absolute clarity.

Pause here.

As you tune in to the feeling of the hand your parent is holding, scan your body. Beginning with the top of your head, feel and sense the energy moving down that side of your body, through your forehead, the eye on that side, the side of your nose, mouth, and jaw. Bring your focus to the arm on that side—your elbow, wrist, hand, and fingers. Scan your body and notice the shoulder on that side, your rib cage, your lung, your hip, leg, and foot. Notice any tensions or injuries you've had there, and you can also notice places that feel good. Notice all you can as you allow yourself to tune in to the idea that the energy on this side of your body is relating to your ancestors. As you do, you can also feel the teeth that relate to that side of the family buzzing with light and healing energy. Allow yourself to be fully aware of the teeth that represent that part of your family. Allow that light to move and flow through you for as long as needed.

Pause here.

When you're ready, allow the other parent to take your other hand. Each parent is standing on the side of your body that represents their lineages. As your other parent takes your hand, allow yourself to be filled with the energy of that family line as well as the other family line. Notice what you notice, feel what you feel.

If there is any discomfort, allow your spirit guide to send healing light to any difficult areas until they feel neutral or peaceful.

Pause here.

When you're ready, release your parents' hands. Thank them again for working with you today and imagine each of them wants to express their sincere thanks and complete gratitude to you for the work you're doing. They are eternally grateful, and they want you to know this is helping the entire family, past, present, and future. Take your time to speak with your parents about anything else they would like to discuss.

Pause here.

Thank them again and say goodbye for now. Your parents are expressing their love; they now walk or float back through the door they came through. Know you will see them again soon.

You're there with your guide. Take a moment to ask your guide for any further clarity or insights you need about this healing.

Pause here.

When you're finished, imagine you can thank your guide for being here today and watch your guide float up, up, up, floating back to where they came from. Know that you will see your guide again soon.

Take a deep breath in through your nose. Breathe in joy, peace, and happiness as you inhale one, two, three, four, and exhale love and light, one, two, three, four. Very good.

Filled with peaceful light, feeling better than you did before, go ahead and turn around now and walk back through the door you came through, back out to where you began your journey. Be there now, back where you began. Close that door behind you and know you will be back there again very soon.

In a moment, when you count from five, you will come back into the room, feeling awake, refreshed, and better than you did before.

Five—grounded, centered, and balanced. Four—continuing to process this new energy in your dreams tonight so by tomorrow morning, you will be fully integrated into these new insights. Three—still surrounded by that beautiful golden ball of light, knowing that only that which is of your highest good can come through, you will find yourself driving carefully and being careful in all activities. Two—grounded, centered, and balanced, and one—you're back.

•• ● ••
JOURNAL PROMPT
Deeper Healing with the Family

Take your time and write down anything important. Here are a few questions to get you going.

1. Did you receive more clarity about which side of your body represents which parent and family lineage?

2. How did it feel to scan your mother's side of your body?

3. How did it feel to scan your father's side of your body?

4. Were you able to recall any tensions or even injuries that you can now see may be related to your ancestors?

5. Were you able to release tensions with the help of your guide?

6. What information did your parents and guide share that you want to recall later?

This process is a journey, not a destination, so if you didn't get much this time, or if you feel you have more to heal than you could possibly get to in one lifetime, please take hope and be encouraged. Making even a little progress in healing is a wonderful step in the right direction. These journeys are peeling back the many layers of the onion of your ancestral history and that will take some time. I applaud you for your progress and efforts.

Cutting Ancestral Cords

Next you will go back into the space where you just were and cut cords between your parents and anything heavy that exists within the body. This is a powerful process and should help relieve any discomfort. Do this when you feel guided.

•• • ••
EXERCISE
Cutting Ancestral Cords

Sit in your sacred space and take a deep, healing breath in through your nose, breathing in love and peace and light. Exhale any tensions and concerns. Continue to breathe, and as you do, you find yourself becoming more and more relaxed. Find yourself breathing in peace, joy, and love as you release tensions and concerns.

Go ahead now and imagine a beautiful beam of pure white light moving through your body from head to feet. Allow the body to receive healing light in every single cell.

Imagine the light is getting stronger now and pours out of your heart center, creating a beautiful golden ball of light that surrounds you by about three feet in all directions. Imagine feeling yourself floating inside this peaceful golden ball of light. Know that within this golden ball of light, you are safe, secure, and totally carefree, and know that within the golden light, only that which is of your highest good can come through.

Walk through the door into your sacred space. Ready? Three, two, one; you're opening the door. Open the door now. Be there now and notice what's happening.

Take your time and bask in the feelings of peace and harmony as you take in all you can. Allow this place to fill your body with light and energy. Become fully refreshed and energized.

Pause here.

As you continue to enjoy your sacred space, imagine your loving guide is floating down to join you now. Feel them land right next to you and imagine they are with you right now. Feel the immense unconditional love they have for you. Know that they are here to support you in this journey.

Let your guide know that you would like to meet your parents again to engage in a deeper healing of the ancestral energy you're carrying within you. As you explain this, your parents are walking through that same door they came through before.

Your parent's Higher Selves are walking or floating up to you now. Say hello and notice they are sending their love and support as well as their eternal thanks to you for doing this work.

Allow one of your parents to approach you and hold the hand that represents their side of the family that lives within your body. As they take your hand, notice the sensations illuminating within you. Scan your body quickly from head to feet, noticing what you notice on that side of your body as it relates to your ancestors. You can easily and more quickly scan your entire head, your eye, half of your nose and mouth and jaw, your shoulder and arm, your rib cage, leg, and foot on the side of the body that is associated with their lineage. Very good.

Imagine your loving guide is approaching you now with a big pair of golden scissors. As they do, you can notice there is an energetic cord of light connecting you and your parent. This light represents the energies of the ancestors and lineage brought to you through your parent. Notice that now and notice how that feels inside your body.

As you do, allow your parent to release your hand while you still notice the energetic cord between the two of you. In a moment, when you count to three, your loving guide will be cutting that cord, releasing all influences from the ancestors and lineage within your body. Ready? One, two, and three, cutting that cord now!

Imagine feeling a beautiful beam of pure white light coming down from above and that light flows through your entire body from head to feet, illuminating the side of the body represented by that parent. Allow your parent to receive this healing too. They are filling with light, and they too are now completely freed from the residual energies of the ancestors and their lineage.

You are both filling with love and light and the side of your body represented by those ancestors and lineage feels wonderful as any tensions disappear and are replaced with light and love.

You and your parent are becoming lighter and lighter and lighter, brighter and brighter and brighter. So light, so bright. You're both feeling better than ever before.

Continue to receive this healing, and when you're ready, imagine that parent moves away.

Pause here.

Once your parent has moved away, they stand on the other side of the room.

Next, your other parent approaches you and holds the hand that represents their side of the family that lives within your body. As they take your hand, notice the sensations illuminating within you. Scan your body quickly from head to feet, noticing what you notice on that side of your body as it relates to your ancestors. You can easily and more quickly scan your entire head, your eye, half of your nose and mouth and jaw, your shoulder and arm, your rib cage, leg, and foot on the side of the body that is associated with their lineage. Very good.

Imagine your loving guide is approaching you now with a big pair of golden scissors. As they do, you can notice there is an energetic cord of light connecting you and your parent. This light represents the energies of the ancestors and lineage brought to you through your parent. Notice that now and notice how that feels inside your body.

As you do, allow your parent to release your hand while you still notice the energetic cord between the two of you. In a moment, when you count to three, your loving guide will be cutting that cord, releasing all influences from the ancestors and lineage within your body. Ready? One, two, and three, cutting that cord now.

Imagine feeling a beautiful beam of pure white light coming down from above, and that light flows through your entire body from head to feet, illuminating the side of the body represented by that parent. Allow your parent to receive this healing too. They are filling with light, and they too are now completely freed from the residual energies of the ancestors and their lineage.

You are both filling with love and light, and the side of your body represented by those ancestors and lineage feels wonderful as any tensions disappear and are replaced with light and love.

You and your parent are becoming lighter and lighter and lighter, brighter and brighter and brighter. So light, so bright. You're both feeling better than ever before.

Continue to receive this healing, and when you're ready, imagine that parent moves away. Notice both of your parents now are filled with more light and love than before. They thank you again for the beautiful work you're doing and send their love, and then, they both walk or float back through the door they came through. Know you will see them again soon.

You're there with your guide. Take a moment to ask your guide for any further clarity or insights about this healing.

Pause here.

When you're finished, imagine you can thank your guide for being here today and watch your guide float up, up, up, floating back to where they came from. Know that you will see your guide again soon.

Take a deep breath in through your nose. Breathe in joy, peace, and happiness as you inhale one, two, three, four, and exhale love and light, one, two, three, four. Very good.

Filled with peaceful light, feeling better than you did before, go ahead and turn around now and walk back through the door you came through and go back out to where you began your journey. Be there now, back where you began. Close that door behind you and know you will be back there again very soon.

In a moment, when you count from five, you will come back into the room, feeling awake, refreshed, and better than you did before.

Five—grounded, centered, and balanced. Four—continuing to process this new energy in your dreams tonight so by tomorrow morning, you will be fully integrated into these new insights. Three—still surrounded by that beautiful golden ball of light, knowing that only that which is of your highest good can come through, you will find your-self driving carefully and being careful in all activities. Two—grounded, centered, and balanced, and one—you're back.

•• • ••
JOURNAL PROMPT
Cutting Ancestral Cords

Once again, take some time to make notes about that journey.

1. How did it feel to cut cords with your mother's lineage?

2. How did it feel to cut cords with your father's lineage?

3. How did you feel overall after doing this journey? Lighter than before? How so?

4. Take any other notes about what you learned while doing this journey.

Next, you will continue this same healing journey with your parents and deepen the experience as you receive more light and release even more unwanted influences.

Taking Out the Trash

Another way to fully remove any heavier energies and unwanted influences is to imagine you can put what isn't serving you out into the trash. The trash container could be a can, a dumpster, anything that has unlimited capacity. Again, you will use your inner vision and healing light to help you release what you don't need and replace that with higher-frequency light and peace.

•• • ••
EXERCISE
Taking Out the Trash

Sit and breathe. Inhale peace and light and exhale tensions. Connect with the bright healing light and allow that to flow through the top of your head, through your entire body, and into your legs and feet. Surround yourself with a golden protective shield of light and know all is well.

Notice the door that leads to your sacred space. When you count back from three, you will walk through that door and go inside your beautiful room. Ready? Three, two, one, you're opening the door. Open the door now. Walk or float inside your beautiful room. Be there now.

Imagine your loving guide is floating down to join you now. Feel them land right next to you. Let your guide know that today you would like to do a deeper healing to take out any residual ancestral influences and remove those from your body.

Imagine your guide can bring out a big dumpster and put it in front of you. Know that this dumpster is unlimited in size so it can hold everything you need to remove.

Notice now also that door where your parents appeared before. The door is opening again, and here come the Higher Selves of your parents. Say hello and allow them to join you at this dumpster. Your parents approach you and hold your hands, the hands that represent their ancestors and lineages. Feel the energizing feeling of connecting to your parents and the love they have for you.

As you enjoy that, when you're ready, let go of their hands and use your hands to reach inside yourself and remove any residual ancestral energies from your mother's side of the family. Take your time as you reach into yourself and imagine you can pull out any heavy energies or emotions that are no longer serving you. Put all these items and energetic forces out of your body and place them into the trash. Know the dumpster holds anything you would like to release. Take your time.

Pause here.

When you feel complete, turn your attention to your father's lineage by focusing on the appropriate side of your body that represents his family. Imagine you can reach into yourself and pull out any heavier or unwanted energies that relate to his lineage and put those out into the trash. Again, take your time to remove all you can at this moment.

Pause here.

When you're finished removing all you can from both your mother and father's sides of the family that reside within you, imagine your loving guide is approaching again with those big golden scissors. Imagine there are cords connecting you with everything in the trash. Those cords and the items in the trash are also connected to your parents.

Beginning with your mother, in a moment, when you count to three, your guide will cut the cords between you and your mother and the items in the trash. Ready? One, two, and three, cutting that cord now. Feel a beautiful healing white light pouring down from above, washing over you and your mother, healing and releasing you from the items in the trash.

Next, turn your attention to your father. Imagine your guide can point out the cords of light connecting you and your father with the items from his lineage that are now in the trash. When you count to three, your guide will cut the cords between you and these unwanted energies. Ready? One, two, and three; your guide is cutting those cords now. You and your father are receiving this loving high frequency as you fully disengage from the items in the trash.

Allow the loving light to wash over you and both your parents. The three of you are getting lighter and lighter and lighter, brighter and brighter and brighter. You're all feeling much better than ever before.

As you continue to receive this healing, your loving guide is lifting that trash and throwing it up into outer space, far away from where you and your family are standing. The trash explodes into stardust. You and your parents are now completely released from any influences and energies from the past.

All of you are becoming brighter and lighter, feeling so much better than before. Take your time to continue to receive this light and love.

Pause here.

When you're ready, imagine your parents once again thank you for your attention to this healing. They are grateful for your help and they both love you more than you can ever imagine. Take a moment to discuss anything else you'd like to talk with them about.

Pause here.

When you're ready, imagine they can say goodbye for now and walk or float back through the door they came through. If needed, you can ask your guide for any further clarity or insights you need about this healing.

Pause here.

When you're finished, imagine you can thank your guide for being here today and watch your guide float up, up, up, floating back to where they came from. Know that you will see your guide again soon.

Take a deep breath in through your nose. Allow yourself to become completely relaxed inside your sacred space. Breathe in the energy of joy, peace, and happiness as you inhale one, two, three, four, and exhale love and light, one, two, three, four. Very good.

Filled with peaceful light, feeling better than you did before, turn around now and walk back through the door you came through and go back out to where you began your journey. Be there now, back where you began. Close that door behind you and know you will be back there again very soon.

In a moment, when you count from five, you will come back into the room, feeling awake, refreshed, and better than you did before.

Five—grounded, centered, and balanced. Four—continuing to process this new energy in your dreams tonight so by tomorrow morning, you will be fully integrated into these new insights. Three—still surrounded by that beautiful golden ball of light, knowing only that which is of your highest good can come through, you will find yourself driving carefully and being careful in all activities. Two—grounded, centered, and balanced, and one—you're back.

• • ● • •

JOURNAL PROMPT
Taking Out the Trash

How did you do? Take a moment to answer the following or make other notes.

1. How did it feel to remove items from your mother's lineage?

2. How did you feel after removing your father's ancestral influences?

3. What did your parents tell you about this?

4. What inner knowing did you receive after doing this process?

5. Could you sense a lightening of your energy after engaging in this way?

6. Note anything else of importance.

Another quick reminder—this is something you may want or need to do more than once. You're peeling back layers of energy relating to events that took place over hundreds and even thousands of years, so just go easy on yourself and progress in your own time and pace.

Fusing the Sides Together

Now that you've worked on the individual sides of the family, another awesome exercise involves bringing both forces together in a new higher-frequency way. You are so unique. You are one in a trillion. Think about that for a moment. You are the one-of-a-kind culmination of all your mother's ancestors, your father's ancestors, the influences of your own past lives, the unique purpose and plan you made for yourself to accomplish in this current lifetime. There is simply nobody else like you, nor will there ever be. You're special.

This next process will be helpful in allowing you to fully embrace, love, and support the unique creation that is you. It feels good to bring everything together as one in a way you have not done before.

•• ● ••
EXERCISE
Fusing the Sides Together

Sit in a comfortable chair with your hands in your lap and feet flat on the floor. Close your eyes. Breathe. Take a deep, healing breath in through your nose, breathing in love and peace and light. Exhale any tensions and concerns. Continue to breathe and as you do, you find yourself becoming more and more relaxed. Imagine a beautiful beam of pure white light coming down through the top of your head. Feel that light moving through your entire body.

Imagine the light is getting stronger now as it pours out of your heart center, creating a beautiful golden ball of light that surrounds you by about three feet in all directions. Imagine feeling yourself floating inside this peaceful golden ball of light. Know that within this golden ball of light, you are safe, secure, and totally carefree, and know that within the golden light, only that which is of your highest good can come through.

Walk through the door into your sacred space where you feel totally relaxed, nurtured, and protected. Ready? Three, two, one, you're opening the door. Open the door now and walk or float inside your beautiful room, a space that you love and enjoy. Be there now.

Imagine your loving spirit guide is there with you and begins now to send a beautiful healing light from above. That light is pouring down through the top of your head, and like a welder's torch, that loving light is fusing together the two halves of your body, bringing peaceful energy and harmony to both sides of your lineage—your mother's and your father's families. The unique energy fuses the two halves of your lineages and merges them together in the one-of-a-kind expression that is you. Allow this merging. Feel or sense the sparks of creation as you fully embrace this newly evolved and heightened sense of your well-being and importance as a soul in the universe at this time.

Breathe. As you do, consciously focus your awareness on your mouth. Bring your lower jaw forward so you can align the edges of your bottom teeth with the edges of your top teeth. Continue to breathe. Feel a pulsating energy rush through your mouth. Imagine you can send light to all your ancestors on both sides of your family through your body and your teeth. Feel heavier energy melting away as you become lighter and lighter and lighter, brighter and brighter and brighter. Continue to allow the teeth that represent your mother's side of the family to merge energies with the teeth representing your father's lineage. Allow that energy to transform into one new and stronger creation. Allow this healing to continue for as long as needed.

Pause here.

When you're ready, take a moment to ask your guide for any further clarity or insights you need about this healing.

Pause here.

When you're finished, imagine you can thank your guide for being here today and watch your guide float up, up, up, floating back to where they came from.

Turn around now and walk back through the door you came through and go back out to where you began your journey. Be there now, back where you began. Close that door behind you and know you will be back there again very soon.

In a moment, when you count from five, you will come back into the room, feeling awake, refreshed, and better than you did before.

Five—grounded, centered, and balanced. Four—continuing to process this new energy in your dreams tonight so by tomorrow morning, you will be fully integrated into these new insights. Three—still surrounded by that beautiful golden ball of light, knowing only that which is of your highest good can come through, you will find yourself driving carefully and being careful in all activities. Two—grounded, centered, and balanced, and one—you're back.

•• ● ••

JOURNAL PROMPT
Fusing the Sides Together

How did you do with that exercise? If you'd like, make a few notes.

1. Were you able to feel the differences between the mother's and father's sides of your body?

2. How did it feel to fuse those two energies together?

3. Did you sense a lightening sensation?

4. How might this new harmonious energy help you in daily life?

Creating a more peaceful union between the alternate lineages embodied within you can be an energizing process. You may want to do this exercise periodically or even regularly for healing and balance.

Healing Past and Future Generations

Next, we will do another short exercise to send healing to your ancestors within your body. For this process, the ancient ones occupy space in your back and future generations of your family energetically reside in the front of your body.

•• ● ••
EXERCISE
Healing Past and Future Generations

Sit in your sacred space and close your eyes. Breathe. Feel that loving and pure bright white light moving through your entire body from head to feet. Surround yourself with the golden protective shield of light and know that within the golden light, all is well.

Go inside your beautiful room and sacred space. Be there now. Your loving guide is floating down to join you. Let your guide know that today you would like to do a deep healing for your ancestors within your body that involves the Frontal Plane.

Stand upright in front of your guide with your feet flat on the floor. Begin to feel your body, and as you do, imagine you can turn your attention to the front of your body, including the top of your head, your forehead, your eyes, nose, mouth, the front part of your neck, your collarbone, your chest and stomach, the front of your rib cage, your legs, kneecaps, the tops of your feet and toes. Send all your energy into those areas now. Take a moment and imagine you can put your full attention into the front of your body.

Pause here.

Very nice. Now when you're ready, move your attention back up to the top of your head. This time, imagine you can bring your energy and awareness into the back of your head and skull, the back of your neck, your shoulder blades, and each vertebra of your spine. Allow your energy and awareness to move down, down, down through every single part of your spine to your tailbone, your buttocks, and down through the backs of your legs, the backs of your knees, your calves, and into the Achilles tendons and soles of your feet.

Pause here.

Next, move your attention from the top of your head, down your back and the backside of your body, but as you do, consider all the ancestors who have gone before you, those who lived hundreds or perhaps even thousands of years before you arrived. Take your time and scan the body, noticing any tensions that may be uncomfortable as well as areas that feel open and peaceful. Go slowly and also notice any thoughts that may come up as you do this process. You're scanning the memories of the past as they may be inside your own energy field, so allow this and notice what you notice, or you may not have any images or memories at all. If not, that's okay. Just allow yourself to scan your back on behalf of your ancestors.

Pause here.

When you're ready and your attention has reached your feet, begin again to notice the top of your head, and this time, allow your energy and attention to move through your forehead, eyes, nose, mouth, and jaw and travel into the front of your body all while considering how your energy feels and the future generations of your family, who will be affected by your energy. Feel this attention as you focus on the front of your neck, your chest, heart, stomach, rib cage in the front of your body, your legs, kneecaps, and so forth. Scan your body and notice any tensions. Observe any ideas or thoughts that come to you. Take your time as you focus on the front of your body until you arrive at the tops of your toes.

Pause here.

Very nice. Next, imagine you can turn your attention to your loving spirit guide or angel. Your guide would like you to know that there is an energetic cord of light that connects you to your ancestors in the back and your future generations in the front. Notice now your guide is carrying a big pair of golden scissors. In a moment, when you count to three, your guide is going to cut the cords of light that exist down your back that are connecting you with all the ancestors from your past. This cutting will release you from any unwanted energies no longer serving you. Ready? One, two, and three, cutting the cords now.

Feel a beautiful healing light moving down the back of your head, through every single cell in your spine; it's continuing to move and work through the back of your rib cage, through your buttocks and the backs of your legs into your Achilles tendons and into the soles of your feet. The light is coming down from above and filling you with peace as you release any energies from the past. You're getting brighter and brighter and brighter and lighter and lighter and lighter. You are filled with peace and light and you may notice that any tense spots in the back of your body are now filled with light, and tensions are going away and gone. Take your time to receive this healing.

Pause here.

Continuing to receive this healing light, you have successfully cut the cords between yourself and the past. Next up, you can turn your attention to the front of the body and imagine your loving guide is still carrying that big pair of golden scissors. In a moment, your guide is going to cut the cord that exists between you and future generations of your family. This cord will represent any energies of disharmony you currently carry, so cutting this cord will provide future generations with the highest energies of love and light possible. In a moment when you count to three, your guide will cut that cord. Ready? One, two, and three; cutting the cord now. A gorgeous beam of light is coming down from above and moving through those cut cords, removing any heavier energies or unwanted influences from you. Your body is filling with light and peace and this new high frequency is pouring from your heart center, beaming out toward the future members of your family. Imagine you can see, feel, or sense the extra love, support, and encouragement this healing is providing to all who have yet to be born within your family. Take your time as you send this love to all.

Pause here.

Now imagine your guide is sending a healing beam of pure white light down through the top of your head. Allow this healing light to fill up every single cell in your entire body, front and back. You are merging the past and future together now as sparks fly and you create a new healing and peaceful vibration of harmony within the past and the future. You're getting lighter and lighter and lighter, brighter and brighter and brighter, so light and so bright. Take your time as you receive this light in all the cells of your body. Imagine this light is aligning your DNA perfectly so you become peaceful, relaxed, and aligned in the highest possible way with your ancestors from the past and future.

Pause here.

Allow this healing to continue as you thank your guide for their assistance today.

Take a moment to ask your guide for any further clarity or insights you need about this healing.

Pause here.

When you're finished, imagine you can thank your guide for being here today and watch your guide float up, up, up, floating back to where they came from. Know that you will see your guide again soon.

Take a deep breath in through your nose. Breathe in one, two, three, four, and exhale one, two, three, and four as you allow yourself to become completely relaxed inside your sacred space. Allow the supportive energies of your sacred space to move through every single cell of your being. As you do, breathe in the energy of joy, peace, and happiness as you inhale one, two, three, four, and exhale love and light, one, two, three, four. Very good.

Filled with peaceful light, feeling better than you did before, go back through the door, out to where you began your journey. Be there now, back where you began. Close that door behind you and know you will be back there again very soon.

In a moment, when you count from five, you will come back into the room, feeling awake, refreshed, and better than you did before.

Five—grounded, centered, and balanced. Four—continuing to process this new energy in your dreams tonight so by tomorrow morning, you will be fully integrated into these new insights. Three—still surrounded by that beautiful golden ball of light, knowing only that which is of your highest good can come through, you will find yourself driving carefully and being careful in all activities. Two—grounded, centered, and balanced, and one—you're back.

How did that feel compared to doing this exercise earlier before you completed all the other family healing experiences? I would imagine it would be quite different. You can do these journeys often to peel back the layers of energy between you and your ancestors and evolve in this healing over time.

•• ● ••
JOURNAL PROMPT
Healing Past and Future Generations

Reflect on the following in your journal.

1. How did it feel to pay attention to your body and acknowledge those who have gone before you and future generations?
2. Did you find the experience differed from what you felt earlier?
3. How did it feel to cut the cords?

This liberating exercise will hopefully give you a sense of increased energy and vitality.

Conscious Cord Cutting

Along those lines, you do not necessarily need to go into a trance to benefit from cutting cords. One of the easier ways to get the hang of this is to simply stand still and quickly cut cords down the front and back of your body anytime, even when you're not in the middle of a guided imagery journey. You can cut the cords easily by simply asking them to be cut between you and all unwanted influences. Use this technique anytime you need to receive greater energy.

• • ● • •

EXERCISE
Conscious Cord Cutting

Here are the steps.

1. Stand upright with your eyes open. Imagine a golden sword comes out in front of you, and starting with the front of your body slightly above your head, the sword is cutting cords between you and any unwanted influences.

2. Then it moves to your back, cutting cords from head to feet.

3. Next, the sword moves down your right side, cutting cords from head to feet and then travels to your left side and cuts any cords from head to feet.

4. Finally, the sword cuts cords by swiping across the top of your head and then moves to the soles of your feet.

5. Imagine that this swiping made a box around your body, and you are now inside a box of high-frequency light, freed of any and all unwanted influences. Imagine you can notice the release of any heavier energies and you feel lighter as a result.

6. Envision yourself inside the protected high-frequency light box and imagine you can carry this with you throughout the day.

And that's it. You can do this anytime for a quick energizing effect. If you choose, you could also sense the healing occurring between past and future generations of your family. It's easy, quick, and powerful.

．． ● ．．

JOURNAL PROMPT
Conscious Cord Cutting

If you experienced anything you want to recall later, here are a few things to consider:

1. How did you feel cutting cords around your body?
2. Did you notice any areas that had greater tension than others?
3. Can you imagine keeping this shield with you throughout the day, and after doing so, did you notice any benefits?

If you like, you could also include ancestral influences as you're doing this, but normally I just ask that any influences be released that are no longer for my highest good, and those could be coming from anywhere, even from things outside my conscious awareness. As with all exercises and guided imagery, do what feels best to you.

Healing All Ancestors within the Cells

Finally, we will do one more energizing exercise to assist you in putting everything together. You've done extensive work with your parents to heal the past and move into the cells of the body to remove unwanted influences and bring the two halves of your family back together in a higher state of alignment. Next, you will energize your cells even more.

．． ● ．．

EXERCISE
Healing All Ancestors within the Cells

Sit in your favorite place. Close your eyes and breathe. Take in healing and light and harmony and exhale tensions.

Connect with a huge bright beam of light and allow that light to flow down from above, moving into your head. Feel that light connecting with every single cell in your head, filling you with light and removing any unwanted energies. That light flows into your eyes, into every cell of the eyes, then into your nose, your ears, your teeth and jaw, your neck. Allow the light to flow through every single vertebra in your neck, healing and transforming all cells and any ancestors residing within you.

That loving light moves from your shoulders into each arm. Feel your right arm as you invite this loving light to flow through your upper arm, into your elbow, forearm, wrist, hand, and right fingers and honor those ancestors represented in the right side of your body. Turn your attention now to your left arm as the loving light flows from your left shoulder into your upper arm, elbow, forearm, hand, and left fingers. Acknowledge the ancestors embodied by the left side of your body.

The light flows through your shoulder, down through your torso and into your legs. Focus on your right leg—your thigh, knee, calf, and right foot, honoring those ancestors now. Turn next to your left leg—thigh, knee, calf, and left foot, also acknowledging the ancestors embodied there.

Continuing to breathe, imagine you can raise the frequency of all the cells in your body. Every single cell is expanding, relaxing, and healing now. You're getting lighter and lighter and lighter, brighter and brighter and brighter. You now feel so light and so very bright that you feel better than ever before.

Surround your entire body with the familiar golden globe of light that protects you and know that your new high-frequency self is totally surrounded and protected within the warm embrace of this golden light, loved unconditionally by your loving ancestors and future generations.

In a moment, when you count back from three, you will return, feeling refreshed and better than ever before.

Three—you're grounded, centered, and balanced. Two—filled with love and peace and light, and one—you're back.

I hope you enjoyed this incredible light-filled journey of peace and hope.

•• ● ••
JOURNAL PROMPT
Healing All Ancestors within the Cells

Take a moment to reflect on that journey.

1. How did it feel to address every cell in your body as a whole and healed unit?

2. Although you already did so much healing work, were you able to sense your energy shifting even higher into a lighter space?

3. Can you see how easy it would be to do this exercise anytime you need added energy?

Consider any other thoughts or feelings that arise from doing this work.

Summing Up

Your ancestors are inside you. Their energy lives within your cells. By utilizing your consciousness and guiding energy directly into the cells of your body, you can remove unwanted influences and heal inherited trauma carried forth from past lineages for the benefit of all future generations of your family.

Conclusion

Henry David Thoreau wrote, "Begin where you are and such as you are, become of more worth, and with kindness aforethought, go about doing good."[19]

I applaud you for the work you've done on behalf of your ancestors. Ancestral Energy Healing is no easy task, as you've discovered. As such, you may not feel at all complete with this process, and I assure you, that is perfectly all right. I feel sure you did good, as Thoreau notes, because of the kindness you've shown to your lineage and because of your pure intention of wanting something better for your ancestors and forthcoming generations.

Because you've done many exercises throughout this book, most of which took place in the theater of your mind, you may wonder what you can expect from the time you've invested during our time together. That's a very good question and one I've asked myself many times. In the earlier part of my career, I would have said healing our ancestors will ensure that we as a collective society will be able to embrace and love each other and make the world a loving place to be.

As time draws on and I am no longer the wide-eyed Pollyanna of my youth, I cannot conclude the same things now that I did in my earlier books. I no longer expect that we can fully escape the difficulties and troubles of daily life on earth. I cannot expect all beings to love

19. Thoreau, *Walden*, 95.

each other unconditionally and problems to magically evaporate before our eyes.

I've come to develop a more realistic view of the world that accepts duality, while remaining ever hopeful that healing our ancestors will enable our beloved up-and-coming generations to better navigate the challenges of the world while remaining here. Problems will still happen, but what if the new understanding people develop could come from their expanded views of reality rather than simply embodying the old models and traumas of thousands of years of human history? It seems that may be the gift. By releasing our ancestral ties and simultaneously honoring those who paved the way for our very existence, future generations can build upon a more positive foundation and expand possibilities for humanity into something that you and I cannot even comprehend from where we're now sitting. That's my hope. Let's heal the collective together and give the gift of expanded consciousness by recognizing the immense capacity for love and good that we're capable of as a human family. Doing so will give our next generation not only a chance, but a glorious purpose for the continuation of our species.

We cannot cling to outcomes. As spiritual people, we know that never works. Rather let's experience this greater room and expanded peace within our own bodies and know that it must be making an impact because we feel it literally in our bones. If you have engaged thus far in any of the practices in the book, you will feel the truth in those words. I'm sure we would all love to time travel into the future to see the effects of our efforts. Since that isn't possible other than to do so within our own imaginations, I will rely on faith. I hope you can do the same and know that this practice and awareness is worth pursuing.

I pray this information will be helpful to you on your path as you gently acknowledge your ancestors in each moment of your life. May greater peace, joy, and love unfold for you and every single member of your beloved clan now and always.

Bibliography

Chapman, Gary D. *The Five Love Languages*. Chicago: North Field Publishing, 2015.

Cowan-Jenssen, Sue. "Prince Harry, Therapy, and Intergenerational Trauma." Welldoing, May 19, 2021. https://welldoing.org/article/prince-harry-therapy-and-intergenerational-trauma.

Ebeling, Florian. *The Secret History of Hermes Trismegistus: Hermeticism from Ancient to Modern Times*. Ithaca: Cornell University Press, 2007.

Henry, Donald O. *Neanderthals in the Levant: Behavioral Organization and the Beginnings of Human Modernity*. New York: Continuum, 2003.

Martinez-Ales, Gonzalo, et al. "Why Are Suicide Rates Increasing in the United States? Towards a Multilevel Reimagination of Suicide Prevention." *Current Topics in Behavioral Neurosciences* 46 (2020): 1–23. doi:10.1007/7854_2020_158.

Morris, Charles R. *The Dawn of Innovation: The First American Industrial Revolution*. New York: Public Affairs Books, 2012.

Oldest. "8 of the Oldest-Known Human Graves in the World." Oldest. https://www.oldest.org/culture/graves/.

Paro, Renato, Ueli Grossniklaus, Raffaella Santoro, and Anton Wutz. *Introduction to Epigenetics*. Cham, Switzerland: Springer Nature, 2021.

Pickering, Craig, et al. "Can Genetic Testing Identify Talent for Sport?" *Genes* 10 (November 26, 2019): 12.972. doi:10.3390/genes10120972.

Rakoff, Vivian M. "A Long-Term Effect of the Concentration-Camp Experience." Jewish General Hospital. University of Toronto Archives and Records Management Services, Reference Code UTA 1682-3-B2015-0011/002(16), 1967. https://discoverarchives.library .utoronto.ca/index.php/long-term-effect-of-concentration-camp -experience-vivian-rakoff-jewish-general-hospital-montreal-article -correspondence-and-background.

Ramirez, Daniel, and Steven A. Haas. "Windows of Vulnerability: Consequences of Exposure Timing during the Dutch Hunger Winter." *Population and Development Review* 48, no. 4 (2022): 959–989. doi:10.1111/padr.12513.

Ross, Christina L. "Energy Medicine: Current Status and Future Perspectives." *Global Advances in Health and Medicine* 8 (February 27, 2019): 2164956119831221. doi:10.1177/2164956119831221.

Sanchez-Roige, S., et al. "The Genetics of Human Personality." *Genes, Brain, and Behavior* 17, 3 (2018): e12439. doi:10.1111/gbb.12439.

Smith, Nicholas J. J. "Time Travel." *The Stanford Encyclopedia of Philosophy* (Fall 2021). https://plato.stanford.edu/archives/fall2021/entries /time-travel.

Spinney, Laura. "Epigenetics, the Misunderstood Science That Could Shed New Light on Ageing." The Guardian, October 10, 2021. https://www.theguardian.com/science/2021/oct/10/epigenetics -the-misunderstood-science-that-could-shed-new-light-on-ageing.

Steiner, Rudolf. *Karmic Relationships: Esoteric Studies VII.* East Sussex, UK: Rudolf Steiner Press, 1973, 2002.

Sundermier, Ali. "99.9999999% of Your Body Is Empty Space." Science Alert, September 23, 2016. www.sciencealert.com/99-9999999-of -your-body-is-empty-space.

Swedan, Nadya. *Women's Sports Medicine and Rehabilitation.* Gaithersburg, MD: Aspen Publishers, 2001.

Thoreau, Henry David. *Walden*. New York: Thomas Y. Crowell & Co., 1910.

Valentine, Tom, Carole Valentine, and Douglas P. Hetrick. *Applied Kinesiology: Muscle Response in Diagnosis, Therapy, and Preventative Medicine*. Rochester, VT: Healing Arts Press, 1985, 1987.

Wolchover, Natalie. "Does Time Really Flow? New Clues Come from a Century-Old Approach to Math." Quanta Magazine, April 7, 2020. https://www.quantamagazine.org/does-time-really-flow-new-clues-come-from-a-century-old-approach-to-math-20200407/.

Yehuda, R., J. Schmeidler, M. Wainberg, K. Binder-Brynes, and T. Duvdevani. "Vulnerability to Post-Traumatic Stress Disorder in Adult Offspring of Holocaust Survivors." *Am J Psychiatry* 155 (1998): 1163–1171.

To Write to the Author

If you wish to contact the author or would like more information about this book, please write to the author in care of Llewellyn Worldwide Ltd. and we will forward your request. Both the author and the publisher appreciate hearing from you and learning of your enjoyment of this book and how it has helped you. Llewellyn Worldwide Ltd. cannot guarantee that every letter written to the author can be answered, but all will be forwarded. Please write to:

Shelley A. Kaehr PhD
℅ Llewellyn Worldwide
2143 Wooddale Drive
Woodbury, MN 55125-2989

Please enclose a self-addressed stamped envelope for reply,
or $1.00 to cover costs. If outside the U.S.A., enclose
an international postal reply coupon.

Many of Llewellyn's authors have websites with additional information and resources. For more information, please visit our website at http://www.llewellyn.com.